Beyond The Scars

Navigating Personal Growth After Trauma

Dr. Lisa M. Wineburg

SKINNY BROWN DOG
MEDIA
EST 2013
ATLANTA | PUNTA DEL ESTE

Published by Skinny Brown Dog Media
Atlanta, GA /Punta del Este, Uruguay

For Information, Contact:
Distributed by Skinny Brown Dog Media
SkinnyBrownDogMedia.com
Email: Info@SkinnyBrownDogMedia.com

Beyond the Scars
Navigating Personal Growth After Trauma
Dr. Lisa M. Wineburg

Library of Congress Cataloging-in-Publication Data
ISBN 978-1-957506-11-1 (eBook)
ISBN 978-1-957506-97-5 (trade paperback)
ISBN 978-1-957506-98-2 (hardcover)
ISBN 978-1-957506-99-9 (case laminate)

Table of Contents

Dedication

This book is dedicated to my younger self, who didn't expect to survive, and all of those like me who have or are struggling to find themselves again after trauma. Know that you can achieve anything with faith, perseverance, and belief in yourself.

More importantly,

*To my loving husband and biggest cheerleader.
Thank you for the love (and tough love), support, guidance and ever-present self-esteem boosts.*

I am eternally grateful.

Epigraph

From trauma's grip, we rise anew,
Scars of battles, proof we've been through,
Yet in the darkness, a flicker of light,
Guiding us toward a future bright.

The fire that once consumed our soul,
Now fuels a fire that makes us whole,
We wear our scars as badges of pride,
A symbol of strength from deep inside.

Our faith tested, but never lost,
In the face of adversity, we paid the cost,
For in the depths of our despair,
We managed to find the strength to repair.

Like a phoenix from the ashes, we re-emerge,
Our stories are rewritten within every surge,
We are warriors and survivors, left temporarily broken,
In our scars lies a valuable message spoken.

United in our overwhelming struggles and strife,
Forever bound by the thread of a resilient life,
We stand tall together, unified as one,
For in our healing, our growth and power have begun.

~ Dr. Lisa M. Wineburg

Introduction

"The greatest source of our suffering are the lies we tell ourselves. They eat away at us and cause us to lose our way as we attempt to navigate through our trauma. The scars left by trauma haunt our souls, especially when we're at our weakest. We struggle to find our identity, for we believe that the "us" of yesterday has disappeared, and we have unwillingly metamorphosized into a lesser, more defeated version of ourselves. This unwanted change can send us on a crash course of painful life lessons that could ultimately lead to a lifetime of endless suffering.

I faced my darkest trauma during my most vulnerable years – as a young child. A time that was supposed to be the age of my innocence soon became a nightmare I couldn't escape. Falling deeper and deeper into self-pity and loathing caused a chain of events that sent me spiraling into a void I thought I would never recover from. I lost my identity, my self-worth, and in some instances, my will to live. I aimlessly wandered through my life numb to the idea of happiness or hope, finding nothing but disappointment and shame along the way.

This is the story of my journey out of the darkness and how I slowly gained strength to find myself, the self I didn't get a chance to discover because the opportunity was taken from me early on. With no support to help navigate the destructive path that resembled my life, I struggled to find my way through the darkness. I gradually crawled through the hopelessness, earning scars and bruises along the way. I fearfully lifted myself up through self-motivation and spiritual renewal, which ignited a fire that ultimately transcended me to what I now call my rebirth. This journey was not easy, but it was necessary for my survival.

This book rested in my soul long before I knew I wanted to write it. In the past, I craved having someone around to feed my spirit as I crawled out of the depths of despair, but it eluded me. Because of this, I reminded myself that when I healed from this anguish, I would reach back and offer my understanding, encouragement, and insight that helped me navigate through the tall weeds to find a safe place to land. Finding solace through building relationships, whether physically or intellectually, through a post-traumatic period can be critical in the recovery phase. For this reason, I have committed myself to executing this through this book and other supportive efforts.

The defining moment for my awakening was around the age of 26 when I saw myself in the mirror one morning after being out all-night drinking. I stared at my reflection, but the girl in the mirror was a stranger. I was in an unfamiliar place without a clue as to how I ended up there. At that moment, I realized the girl I saw wasn't me; she was a broken, darker version of me. She was a hurt, self-deprecating, self-sabotaging, lost soul who craved validation from the wrong people and places. This, in turn, caused a destructive recurring episode for years to come with no end in sight. I soon realized I was becoming someone I despised and decided enough was enough. This sparked an uprising inside of me and created a desire to release myself from the trauma weighing me down.

As we embark on this journey of self-discovery after trauma, we should be reminded that no trauma is created equal, and everyone's journey has its own winding roads. What is constant is that we all can find our own path to redemption. We need to take the steps that lead us there, regardless of the level of difficulty or how long it takes. The key is never to give up and incessantly fight for your right to heal your scars, grow, and become the powerful person you were destined to be. Finding your way through trauma may seem daunting, but you must believe that while it can be challenging, it's not impossible.

We will explore the mechanics of trauma and ways to navigate its damaging effects, but before we delve into this exploration, we must identify a few key things. We must acknowledge that the trauma exists and understand that we can't downplay or escape it. We must embrace these truths to confront our trauma head-on and begin the healing process. Healing comes with learning helpful ways to process your feelings, identify triggers, and rewire your thinking related to trauma and healing. Addressing these areas sets you on the path of unearthing your restored confidence to initiate your pursuit of self-discovery through post-traumatic growth. Together, we will build the tools necessary to achieve a higher level of consciousness and ignite a fire inside you that will empower you to take your own journey.

To begin healing from trauma, we must first acknowledge it and then begin to move toward a place of resolution. This step may seem complicated, but the sheer fact that you are still standing shows you are resilient, and now it's time for your posttraumatic growth. Growth is different from resilience in that resilience helps you to survive; growth will help you to move forward with your life. This growth evolves, leaving the stain of trauma behind you as a notion of what happened to you and not the definition of you. Once you are ready for the growth stage, you will begin to understand who you are and, gradually, what you need to do to become whole once again. You will learn how to take control of your life and create ownership of your future.

In my discovery of self-love and strengthening my foundation, I realized that I had developed a helping spirit; I had become a nurturer, if you will. My desire to nurture others grew into a passion that led me to become a mental health therapist. From the beginning, I flourished in my profession and knew immediately that it was my destiny and God's calling for me. It became a way for me not only to help heal but to continue my healing through helping. For the first time, I knew what my purpose on this earth was, to help others navigate through the muddy waters we call life and help them to see their life beyond the scars.

This book will not cure your ailments in itself; you must put in the work. I will not hold your hand and walk you through the pain, but I will give you encouragement and guidance. I will lead you to discover new heights and new beginnings that are essential to rebuilding. While this book is not the end all be all of the healing process, it is a place to take a deep breath, let out a big sigh, and begin the voyage to a post-traumatic destiny. Together, we can build a game plan and set you on a course for rediscovery with a new purpose and appreciation for life. Join me on this journey, and together, we'll unlock the keys to overcoming our past, taking charge of our present, and embracing a future of post-traumatic growth and self-discovery.

"Trauma teaches us that healing is not about forgetting; it's about embracing our scars and using them as reminders of our strength and resilience."

~ Dr. Christine A. Courtois

CHAPTER 1

Understanding Post-Traumatic Growth

▌ Introduction to Trauma

In the dictionary, trauma is defined as a lasting emotional response that often results from living through a distressing event. In other words, trauma is a deep psychological wound that can come from a variety of negative experiences. It often leaves a lasting effect on a person's emotional and mental health. Whether it be physical or emotional abuse, the loss of a loved one, or even witnessing a traumatic event, the effects of trauma can be profound and far-reaching. It is important to recognize that trauma goes beyond temporary discomfort. It strikes at the core of our well-being, leaving behind scars that may never fully heal. It leaves us trapped in an emotional tailspin with what seems like no way out.

There are three main types of trauma: acute, chronic, and complex. Acute trauma refers to a single traumatic event that occurs within a short period of time. This could include incidents such as accidents, natural disasters, or acts of violence. Chronic trauma, on the other hand, refers to repeated and prolonged exposure to traumatic events over an extended period. This can occur in situations such as ongoing abuse, domestic violence, or living in war-torn areas. Complex trauma involves exposure to multiple and varied traumatic experiences over time. It often occurs during childhood and can result from prolonged abuse or neglect within the family system. Each type of trauma, whether a single episode or repeated trauma exposure, can have damaging effects and can be challenging to overcome. It can affect our ability to form healthy relationships, maintain a job, or engage in activities we once enjoyed. They produce unwanted triggers that add to the agony we are already experiencing.

Acute trauma often triggers a fight-or-flight response, leading to symptoms like increased heart rate, rapid breathing, and heightened anxiety. Some may also experience confusion, disorientation, or numbness in the aftermath of the event. In addition to these immediate effects, acute trauma can have lasting impacts on mental health. Chronic and complex trauma both lead to a range of symptoms that may affect us physically, emotionally, and mentally. Physical symptoms of chronic trauma may include headaches, digestive issues, chronic pain, or discomfort in the body. Emotionally, we may experience intense feelings of panic, grief, anger, or shame. We might also struggle with difficulties in regulating our emotions and have a heightened sense of alertness and hypervigilance. Mental symptoms can vary from problems with concentration and memory loss to experiencing intrusive thoughts or flashbacks related to traumatic events. Regardless of the type of trauma we have experienced, it leaves us unable to travel the emotional landscape that it causes, leaving us exiled.

▌ The Emotional Landscape of Trauma

When we experience a crisis or traumatic event, we feel no good will ever come from it. We feel that there is no way to get past its destruction. It may seem that we are trapped in a darkness that no one could possibly comprehend. This leaves us feeling alone and scared, isolated from the world we so desperately long to be a part of. Its impact can be profound and long-lasting, affecting various aspects of our lives, such as our emotions, thoughts, behaviors, and relationships. It's important to recognize that trauma is a complex experience that affects all of us differently. While some people may be able to cope with traumatic events relatively well, others may struggle significantly in their ability to process and recover from them.

For some, traumatic events can lead to difficulties in daily functioning. It can cause emotional distress, intrusive thoughts, and changes in our mood. These experiences can make it challenging for us to concentrate, make decisions, or engage in usual activities. We may experience fear, sadness, anger, or guilt following a traumatic event. Experiencing these symptoms can lead to sleep disturbances such as insomnia or nightmares, which can disrupt regular sleep patterns and contribute to feelings of exhaustion and fatigue during the day. Insomnia refers to difficulty falling asleep or staying asleep throughout the night. Nightmares, on the other hand, are vivid and distressing dreams that often wake us up during the night. Both can have a profound effect on daily life and may cause you to have difficulty restoring balance in your life.

These responses may arise due to the shock and disbelief of what has occurred or as a result of processing the event's consequences. It is not uncommon for feelings of shock and disbelief to arise when faced with unexpected or traumatic events. These emotions can stem from the suddenness or severity of the circumstances, leaving us feeling overwhelmed and unable to fully comprehend what has happened. It may take time for the shock to subside and for us to come to terms with the reality of the situation. This is when we can start to take stock of our emotional state and decide what to do next. Are we resilient enough to make it through? Are we in a place to begin the journey of post-traumatic growth? Do we know what any of this means? Let's take this opportunity to better understand what this means and how we make that journey.

Introduction to Resilience and Post-Traumatic Growth

While the journey through these emotions is challenging, it can also lead to an unexpected destination: Post-traumatic growth. While some may think the act of being resilient is the same as post-traumatic growth, they are mistaken. Resilience refers to an individual's remarkable capacity to not only recover but also thrive following a traumatic experience. It is the extraordinary ability to bounce back with ease, adapt to new circumstances, and maintain emotional well-being despite the difficulties faced. Resilience encompasses various psychological and emotional processes that enable us to cope effectively with stressors, cultivate positive coping strategies, and foster personal growth in the face of adversity.

By developing resilience skills and utilizing them during challenging times, individuals can overcome obstacles and emerge stronger than before. This ability is not afforded to everyone. It involves maintaining a positive attitude, managing emotions effectively, and finding ways to navigate challenges with determination. While some individuals may naturally possess more resilience than others, it is important to note that resilience is not an inherent trait but rather a skill that can be refined.

Post-traumatic growth, on the other hand, is a psychological phenomenon that refers to the positive changes that individuals may experience after going through a traumatic event. It is the concept that we can recover from our trauma and grow and thrive in various aspects of our lives. This growth can manifest in several ways: increased personal strength, enhanced relationships, greater appreciation for life, a deeper sense of purpose, and improved resilience to future challenges. It is important to note that post-traumatic growth does not negate or diminish the pain and suffering experienced during the traumatic event but rather highlights the potential for personal transformation and psychological resilience in the aftermath. Both resilience and post-traumatic growth require a dedication to healing. Nonetheless, they are two separate approaches.

Resilience vs. Post-Traumatic Growth: Recognizing the Difference

Before beginning our voyage on the path to self-discovery, we must take a moment to take a deeper dive into differentiating between resilience and post-traumatic growth. Often, we confuse posttraumatic growth for resilience and convince ourselves that our work is done once the trauma is over. We mindlessly believe we can sweep the incident under the rug and move on with our lives without dealing with the aftermath. This is where we are mistaken. While both are essential tools in moving through trauma, they are two totally different levels of consciousness. Resilience or "strength" is what we need to make it through the trauma as it unfolds, and posttraumatic growth happens after we have survived the trauma and recognize it for what it is. It is instrumental in sparking the positive change that helps us move forward, shedding the heaviness trauma causes. In essence, resilience focuses on adapting and adjusting to the trauma, and posttraumatic growth focuses on positive transformative changes that help you to move out of the guilt or fear to discover what your life could be like once you are detached from the trauma. I like to call this moment the "detach and detangle phase."

The detach and detangle phase is a process many of us think we understand, but we are sometimes misled. To truly accomplish this goal, we must work hard to sever deeply rooted ties that we have become dependent upon. These ties have become our way of life and dissolving them can often leave us dazed and confused. This can send us into a tailspin, not knowing how to pick up the pieces. Nonetheless, we must cut these debilitating restraints that keep us bound and break free from the negative energy that is associated with trauma. Detaching will give you the emotional space you need to allow yourself the opportunity to take care of yourself and refocus your efforts on the future. To detach means avoiding specific people or situations that constantly cause you stress or anxiety, and it allows you to create boundaries to protect your mental and emotional well-being. There is no timeline for learning how to detach yourself from harmful customs. Just make sure you consciously and actively work on cutting the strings holding you captive from achieving your post-traumatic growth.

Detangling comes once you have found the strength to detach yourself from the chaos of negative energy. Detangling encompasses straightening out or clearing up anything that is confusing, worrying, or complex. Detangling comes in many forms and is also essential to your growth. Once the strings are cut, you will begin to detangle your life in ways that promote self-love and self-discovery. Some ways to straighten out your life include clearing up your old and negative thoughts & beliefs, creating new standards for how you want to live your life, discovering who you are again, and making clearly defined plans for navigating your future as you move forward. You have gained the strength and insight to detach from the trauma, and now it's time to detangle the feelings and emotions to release you further from its grasp. Finding the courage to detach and detangle from things and people that hinder our progress is at the center of posttraumatic growth. While having the courage to endure trauma demonstrates resilience, taking these additional steps leads to growth.

Real-Life Illustrations: Resilience and Growth in Action

You may be scratching your head and saying, "I'm still confused; it still seems like resilience and post-traumatic growth are the same." Don't worry; I can see why you would come to this conclusion, so here is an example of resilience versus posttraumatic growth. Consider this scenario: Someone has been in an unhealthy relationship for several years. In this relationship, they endured physical, mental, and emotional pain caused by their significant other. One day, they decided to join a support group to better understand why they remained in this toxic relationship. They learn through these sessions that they are not stuck, in fact, they can leave at any time. After several sessions, they gain courage and decide to leave the relationship. They discover that their life can be whatever they want it to be and turn their horrible experience into a learning experience. You see, the person showed resilience in that they endured what was happening to them, learned to adapt to the toxic environment, and eventually decided to go to therapy. They were in survival mode. The post-traumatic growth came when they realized they had options and found the will to leave the relationship, which permitted them to move their life forward.

I recall early on in my practice, a 16-year-old client, feeling hopeless and broken, came to me for therapy at her mother's suggestion. She had a traumatic encounter with her 17-year-old male cousin, who molested and raped her one evening at a family gathering. The event was so horrific that she couldn't force herself to speak about it for months. Although devastated by the encounter, she somehow fought to maintain a 4.0-grade point average in school because she knew it was important to her future. However, she was isolated and withdrawn from her family and social life, struggling to maintain her sanity daily. She showed resilience in that she managed to survive the incident and attempted to maintain something that would be important to her future success: school. Still, she didn't have the strength to fight for the normalcy and happiness that was once a part of her life. Reluctantly, she agreed to therapy with me, and after six difficult weeks of treatment, the fun-loving, confident teenager she once was started to emerge again. She soon began to see life through a different lens and accepted what happened to her as misfortune, not the thing that defined her. She was starting to experience post-traumatic growth, and once she recognized it, she was unstoppable.

Now that you have a clear understanding of the two, it's time to take ownership of your trauma and put one foot in front of the other. Let's take a walk into the unknown, a place that is filled with hope and renewal. While the unknown can be a scary place, it can also be a place of restoration. A place you can make your own stocked with all of the encouragement, happiness and support you could ever need. Take comfort in the unlimited possibilities you'll discover on the journey you are about to embark on. Let's not be afraid of the unknown but embrace its allure, for our future lies in the place where the unknown begins.

The Unexpected Evolution of Post-Traumatic Growth

Post-traumatic growth is not just about surviving trauma; it's about transforming and thriving. This may include gaining new perspectives, strengthening relationships, or discovering unique inner strengths. When we allow time for reflection, it can be eye-opening. These small moments allow us the opportunity to gain insight into how we are really doing. It is in these quiet, uninterrupted moments that clarity occurs. Even during the most trying times, it is visible. It grants us a small window to gaze into our innermost thoughts and a door to release our innermost pain. Through this act of self-reflection, we experience personal growth, whether expected or unexpected. Without warning, our mind, body and soul adjust to the shifts and follow the natural flow of progress. While we may initially try to resist growth, believing it is too soon, we must embrace change as it comes. We unwillingly try to fight against growth because it seems like it's too soon or that maybe we are not ready. In reality, we are ready, and the change is occurring right on time. That's how growth happens; it comes out of thin air and surrounds us with a sense of hope and possibility. We find comfort in our growth once we can identify it. The hardest part is getting to a breakthrough and allowing it to manifest itself into something extraordinary.

The unexpected evolution of post-traumatic growth can be shocking and unfamiliar. Don't be afraid of it; embrace it. Find yourself again and allow for upgrades to the new you. Shed the dead weight of insecurity and shame and allow your inner peace to soar. Let your conscience be your guide and follow your instincts when it comes to harnessing your strength. Remember, positive changes often happen when you least expect them. View them as signs of progress rather than resistance. Take it day by day and focus on the small things. A handful of small things turn into significant changes. Be open and receptive to the unknown forces that align when you reach your evolutionary phase. Have faith in your ability to grow and heal. Be strong, be vigilant, and be receptive, for change is inevitable if you stay the course and follow your heart.

Theoretical Foundation: The Science Behind Growth

Several theories support the human pursuit of healing and recovery during difficult times. Each has different ideologies on how they interplay with human development and the ability to change. One theory that explains the positive transformation in the aftermath of trauma is the Post-Traumatic Growth (PTG) theory. It was developed by psychologists Richard Tedeschi, Ph.D., and Lawrence Calhoun, Ph.D., in the 1990s, concluding that people who suffer psychological difficulty following trauma can often see positive growth afterward. It goes on to explain that people develop a new understanding of themselves, the world they live in, and the possibilities for their future. Finding this type of enlightenment strengthens our resolve to change and allows the necessary transformation of a positive evolution to take place. This makes post-traumatic growth essential in overcoming our trauma and healing from its life-changing influences.

Alongside PTG, there are other theories that explain the human condition and how it relates to promoting growth. A few include concepts such as Resilience Theory (RT) and Trauma and Recovery Model (TRM). Resilience theory focuses on the ability of people to bounce back from adversity and resume normal functioning. As mentioned previously, RT works with the concept of resilience and its propensity to provide a person refuge while experiencing trauma. Resilience is what keeps people in survival mode, which allows them to endure the ordeal and make it to the other side. While RT focuses on the principles of how people rebound from trauma, TRM delves into the stages of reclaiming life after trauma. Both transcend any notion that healing is an option that is attainable without achieving pre-post traumatic growth.

Trauma occurs in three main stages:

1. Safety, Stabilization and Engagement, which engage and empower you and build your internal and external resources and support.

2. Processing of Traumatic Memories, which is used to purposefully draw attention to traumatic memories and their emotional distress in order to increase a sense of control over the trauma.

3. Lastly, it focuses on Developing a Sense of Personal Well-being, which incorporates and strengthens skills and knowledge and increases self-awareness to enhance personal well-being.

It is in this last phase that post-traumatic growth can be explored. It allows time to acknowledge that while trauma is undesirable, those who survive report a new level of resilience, additional survival skills, greater self-appreciation, increased empathy, and a broader view of life in general.

While the theoretical aspect of growth is the last thing we think of, it resonates in our actions. Reflection, thought-changing, and resilience are all a part of the growth process. The theoretical perspective of human nature is what unconsciously guides us in our recovery process. We utilize these aspects of transformation to nurture us and lift us out of the depths of anguish. Seldom do we think about what leads us through this process, but rest assured, it's contributed to the science of it all. There are three critical components to development. Growth involves physically getting larger through changes in our thought processes; maturation, which involves the physical, emotional, or intellectual development of our soul; and learning, which involves changing thoughts, behaviors, or emotions, which are based on environmental factors and our desire to evolve. These are all tools for growth that help to catapult us into recovery from trauma.

▌ Physiological and Behavioral Responses to Trauma

Another helpful tool for healing during post-traumatic growth is processing your emotions. Emotional processing will help tie together many pieces you may not believe are connected, such as your body's physiological and behavioral responses to trauma. Psychological impairments are not the only symptoms generated by trauma, and many of us may not be aware that these other symptoms occur as a result of a traumatic experience. We believe that these responses are caused by illness or experiencing a bad day; however, they can actually be a direct response to the residual effects of trauma. For instance, physiological responses to trauma can include persistent fatigue, sleep disorders, nightmares, fear of recurrence of the trauma, anxiety, flashbacks, depression, and avoidance of emotions or activities that are associated with the trauma.

These physical irregularities can go unnoticed or be medically associated and tied to trauma. Therefore, recognizing physiological responses is an important step in our healing process. The body's behavioral responses to trauma can include restlessness, sleep and appetite disturbances, difficulty expressing yourself, increased use of drugs and alcohol, and a decline in stable relationships. All of these symptoms can be linked to trauma, so we must be aware of the not-so-obvious correlation. The connection between mind and body is powerful, so it is essential to be mindful of every sensation, irregularity, and disturbance within our bodies and thoughtfully address them, whether you feel it's related to the trauma or not.

Psychosomatic responses are not always related to a physical ailment. Sometimes, they can indicate a direct response to the residual effects of trauma. Trauma's aftermath can alter not only your physical and emotional outcomes but also your mental stability. Understanding how trauma manifests in the body and mind is crucial for identifying triggers that can decide how quickly and effectively you heal. Our innate ability to adapt to adversity can be a lifesaver when transitioning through a traumatic event. The ability to recognize physiology and behavioral responses is paramount to achieving post-traumatic growth and promoting lifelong self-discovery.

▌ The Positive Outcomes of Post-Traumatic Growth

Despite an event's difficulty, overcoming negative experiences can bring about positive change through post-traumatic growth. Some changes include discovering personal strengths, identifying new possibilities, forging and improving relationships, gaining a greater appreciation for life, and spiritual growth. To successfully navigate these changes, you must process your emotions and identify triggers that can possibly hinder your post-traumatic growth and remove them. Even after you reach your own level of post-traumatic growth, you're still going to have bad days, and you're still going to be reminded of how difficult those times were in your darkest hour. Still, you will be empowered to persevere and not allow the bad memories of the past to interfere with your growth. You will learn to forge ahead, find the strength to live your life and serve your purpose as it was intended.

When we reach our growth, we manage to find the ability to reflect on the long-term effects of traumatic events. We discover that the outcomes encompass both good and bad changes. If we are so fortunate as to recognize and reflect on both of these outcomes, we have begun to embark on our journey to posttraumatic growth. We shift our mindset to see the potential for light amid the darkness. This process becomes our beacon of light. It steers us to a path of enlightenment and healing. It is this forward motion that allows us to transcend to a place where we are reborn and can live again. We begin to see the light at the end of the tunnel eventually. We learn that even horrifying events have the potential to inspire growth and strength within us that we never deemed possible.

Post-traumatic growth relies on a strength you never thought you would ever need. It is discovered by reaching deep down inside and finding small bits and pieces of yourself that crave the will to thrive outside the realms of trauma. The realms of trauma can be suffocating and take an insurmountable toll on your thirst to live. It can leave you hopeless and block out any waves of perseverance necessary to succeed. This is why processing your emotions, identifying triggers, and realizing that there can be some positive changes as a result of trauma can be essential to enhancing your overall perception. While it may seem impossible to reach this goal, it only takes having the will. By digging deep within ourselves, we can uncover the potential for growth that trauma tries to smother. We must nurture the seedling of positivity trying to sprout, using its strength to spark an uprising.

There is a new person waiting to be born inside of that rotten shell we call trauma. A person full of life, dreams, and aspirations. A person who has decided not to allow their pain and suffering to continue to swallow them whole. A person ready to shed the burdens that control their world. It's time to nurture and nourish this seedling with positivity, love, and motivation. Let's allow it to grow strong by absorbing all of the good surrounding it and using its strength to cause an uprising. An uprising that sets your inner soul on fire and inspires you to take the next steps into a world of unimaginable possibilities. It's time to take back control and welcome the necessary change for a brighter tomorrow.

▍ Embracing the Journey Ahead: A Reflection

As we draw this chapter to a close, let's take a moment to journey back through the landscapes we've traversed. We began in the shadowed valleys of trauma, where feelings of isolation and despair often loom large. Yet, even in these depths, we've seen a glimpse of the potential for growth and the spark of newfound strength. We walked the line between resilience, which is that enduring spirit that helps us weather the storm. And learned that post-traumatic growth is the transformative change that comes after the storm has passed. Through the stories of real lives, we felt the tangible heartbeat of these concepts, understanding their differences and their intertwined dance.

We can now differentiate resilience and post-traumatic growth, which will help us when navigating our healing process. We understand that healing is unique and that we must not lose sight of hope. Keeping hope's light in view, we must stay the course and be vigilant in our pursuit of renewed happiness. The emotional landscape of trauma will appear too difficult to navigate at times. It may start out as rough, winding terrain that may cause you to lose your footing. It inspires doubt but we push ahead blocking out trauma's hostile whispers. Eventually, the road transforms into a scenic route where roses bloom, releasing us from alternate realities.

While the idea of breaking free from the chains of trauma may sometimes seem elusive, it is not out of your reach. If we can train our focus on identifying that there are both good and bad changes that emerge through our trauma, we will be set free. It is just a matter of time, and quite frankly, it is all within your control. You are the powerful force that will awaken your inner strength. You also have the power to unlock the shackles of despair and fear and walk in the footsteps of hope and faith. You have the power to say I will no longer live in this land of sorrow and pain. You have the power to say, " I am worthy," and " I will not let this define me." You are the decider of your fate and the leader of your destiny. It is you who has the ability to give yourself permission to take the journey down the road of self-discovery. It is only you who can make it happen, and it can happen if you have faith and trust in the process.

Now that we have set the record straight, we will embolden ourselves to take the next logical steps to our journey of self-discovery. While we now understand that though trauma is painful, confusing, and sometimes debilitating both mentally and physically, we will find strength from within to heal and move on. We also recognize that the mind and body are connected and feed off of one another, controlling who we are and how we experience things. Because of this interconnectedness, we must now become vigilant of the physical, psychological, and behavioral signs caused by trauma. Having this knowledge gives us power; having this power makes us stronger, and that strength is what creates growth. We must unsubscribe from the idea that being resilient is enough and welcome the necessary changes that allow us to walk confidently into our journey of post-traumatic growth.

As we stand at this chapter's end, looking back at the terrain we've covered, I invite you to reflect: Where do you see yourself in this landscape? Have you felt the enduring spirit of resilience? Or perhaps you've begun to feel the transformative winds of post-traumatic growth? Understanding trauma and the potential for post-traumatic growth sets the foundation for our journey. In the next chapter, we will explore how to navigate the darkness that trauma often brings. We will delve into strategies and techniques that will assist us in navigating through this darkness. By exploring different coping mechanisms and approaches, we hope to provide valuable insights into how one can effectively deal with the aftermath of traumatic events. Remember, every journey toward healing is unique, but understanding trauma and embracing the potential for growth are essential steps in finding light among the darkness.

If you continue to carry bricks from your past,
you will end up building the same house.

~Unknown

CHAPTER 2

Navigating the Darkness

Part 1: The Immediate Aftermath

❚ Understanding the Immediate Emotional Response

Trauma plunges us into a period of darkness, manifesting as confusion, fear, and a sense of loss. Experiencing trauma profoundly disrupts our stability, leaving us feeling vulnerable. It shatters our beliefs, overwhelming us with unanswerable questions that deepen confusion. This bewilderment further distresses an already difficult situation. Though disorienting, we must remember that confusion is a natural response when seeking an understanding of the inexplicable.

The confusion we experience can add an additional layer of distress to an already difficult situation. It is important to remember that this is a normal reaction to such experiences. Our minds naturally seek understanding and meaning, but sometimes, the answers may not be immediately apparent or easily accessible. Our thoughts and emotions are in disarray. It can feel as though we are trapped in a fog of uncertainty, unable to make sense of our own experiences This can lead to feelings of frustration, helplessness, and even self-blame. But it's essential to remember that this confusion does not define us or our ability to heal. It is merely a natural response to a traumatic event.

Fear also frequently follows trauma, creating ongoing anxiety for safety. Life-threatening events breed debilitating fears of recurrence triggering traumatic memories. While valid, these fears need not control us. It's important to recognize that these fears are valid responses to what you have been through, but they don't have to control your life. Furthermore, trauma disconnects us from our sense of self, evoking grief for who we were before. Such identity loss is a typical traumatic response. Amid the darkness, it signals the onset of a painful yet hopeful healing process, guiding us slowly into the light.

Navigating through the darkness can be a daunting task. Somedays, you feel like you are finally seeing the light at the end of the tunnel; in others, you feel like someone gut-punched you into the depths of despair. I'm here to tell you that it will get better and that you just need to hold on to the promise that tomorrow brings. It can seem pointless to stay optimistic, but optimism is the path to redemption. We all struggle to process trauma's senseless anguish, yet inherently,

we can restore and heal ourselves. This uncomfortable transformation needs occasional encouragement and guidance to unlock happiness again. First, acknowledge the suffering ahead. Then resolution can begin.

Consider my story, which illustrates this turbulent period distinctly. My vivid darkness illustrates such shaking challenges. I once operated solely on hatred, shunning kind gestures. Trauma consumed me, morphing me into someone unrecognizable—rude, dismissive, disdainful. My unconscious suit of armor simultaneously guarded yet buried me until its inexplicable collapse—the awakening. I could no longer tolerate this delusional alternate reality and had to rediscover my true self. There wasn't a person on this earth that I could trust or confide in; I navigated my world alone. When people tried to befriend me, I immediately scoffed at the idea. How could I possibly be friends with them? They only want access to me to take advantage of me. This led to the dismissal of friends or the dissolution of comradery before its inception. When someone offered kind words or gestures, I almost instinctually met them with a tone of spite. I was possessed by a spirit of hostility that became my identity. I soon became the person to steer clear of in everyone's eyes and I savored it. The putrid stain of my trauma consumed me, and I transformed before my very eyes into the monster that was fueled by my trauma.

After years of wandering in a self-created traumatic hell—disconnected, disdainful—I transformed into someone unrecognizable, dreadful. This illusion of armor entombed me until an epiphanic awakening stopped that illusion. I was determined to step out and rediscover reality, my true self. Though revelation struck instantly, the messy healing path lurched unpredictably between setbacks and victories. Still, I persevered. Occasional backslides occurred; after all, I'm human. But consistency catalyzes success—not the pursuit of excellence. Inching ahead with self-compassion slowly revealed progress within me.

Realizing the need to heal was straightforward yet embarking on that path proved challenging. Throughout my healing journey, there were moments when it felt insurmountable, but that perception was mistaken. The old saying holds, "It's always darkest before the dawn," which resonated deeply with me. My inner battles were fierce, with my demons clinging tightly, leaving me void of release. Progress often felt like two steps forward and eight back, plunging me into a sense of defeat. Despite the struggle, my resolve never wavered; I persistently pushed through the difficulty. Naturally, there were times when I faltered, reverting to past unhealthy behaviors—such is the human condition. It's crucial to acknowledge that faltering is part of the process. What matters is that you rise, shake off the dust, and step forward once more. After all, it is consistency, not perfection, that paves the way to triumph.

Navigating the aftermath of trauma is akin to finding your way in the dark. Healing is not straightforward—it's a journey marked by fluctuating progress and occasional setbacks. In our darkest times, it's crucial to remember the power of consistency in our healing efforts. Being consistent means being present for ourselves daily, even when it's tough or feels overwhelming. Recognizing that healing is a gradual process is vital; some days, progress may seem negligible. Yet, every step, no matter how small, is valuable and contributes to our healing. As we move through the shadows cast by trauma, let's adopt consistency as our guiding light. With time and commitment, we'll discover the resilience to heal and forge a hopeful future.

Part 2: Seeking Paths to Healing

▌ Finding Your Path to Healing

As you let consistency illuminate your path, it's time to embrace healing. Here are some guiding principles to aid you. Understand that healing is a unique journey without a universal roadmap. You might begin with a strategy to confront your trauma directly, which is commendable. Follow your initial plan, knowing it's a starting point. However, expect challenges—don't be disheartened by unforeseen 'avalanches' that may obstruct your path. Instead, regroup and seek alternative routes. Consider such disruptions as life's common hurdles; by anticipating them, their impact diminishes.

Preparing for life's 'avalanches' means cultivating resilience and a proactive mindset. This foresight allows us to handle obstacles with greater ease. Forewarned is forearmed; by expecting the unexpected, we maintain composure when faced with setbacks, thus reducing their stress-inducing effects. Facing life's tribulations head-on is seldom simple, but with problem-solving skills and the support of confidants, we can navigate any challenge. Sharing our struggles can provide fresh insights and much-needed encouragement. Maintaining a positive outlook transforms these challenges into opportunities for growth. Let's draw upon our inner fortitude and confront these 'avalanches' with courage. With such tenacity, there's nothing we can't overcome.

A pivotal tip for your healing journey is to practice self-compassion. Grant yourself the grace to accept missteps. As I've mentioned, our shared humanity means we are prone to mistakes. Allowing space for these errors, and forgiving yourself for them, is crucial for maintaining your resolve to continue. This path to post-traumatic growth is a relentless fight; enduring it requires arming yourself with focus, fortitude, forgiveness, and faith. Focus sharpens our awareness, fortitude gives us strength, forgiveness is self-explanatory, and faith instills the belief that we will prevail.

Setting attainable goals is also vital for navigating the path to post-traumatic growth. Realistic aims provide a blueprint for our healing and offer direction. These milestones, which vary according to our personal goals and challenges, empower us. They act as beacons of progress, whether they involve acquiring new skills or overcoming specific obstacles. Venturing outside our comfort zones promotes growth and resilience. It's essential to set goals that align with your current reality, allowing you to celebrate frequent victories that bolster your overall development.

Equipped with these strategies, you must now gather additional tools to ensure victory in your healing. While the aforementioned tactics will aid your journey through trauma, it's equally important to ward off the encroaching darkness. Complacency is a subtle enemy, and vigilance is its antidote. Adopting proactive, daily strategies to find meaning and purpose fortifies us against adversity. By identifying and embracing these practices, we keep ourselves content and in command of our progress. Darkness may prowl, seeking to undo our gains, but our unwavering vigilance and determination are its annoyance.

Part 3: Tools for the Journey

▌ Tools to Maintain Progress on Your New Journey

To ensure your progress continues to ascend, consider integrating several key practices into your routine. Journaling is one I highly encourage. It's a potent strategy for organizing your thoughts, mapping out plans, setting priorities, and monitoring your journey. Reflecting on past journal entries can be incredibly affirming; it allows you to appreciate the distance traversed or recognize areas needing further growth. Keeping a journal is a great way to clear your mind of thoughts you're continuously holding on to and allowing them to live elsewhere.

Positive affirmations are another powerful tool. Placing encouraging notes around your living space, like "You can do anything you set your mind to," can offer daily empowerment. This practice might seem trivial, but its uplifting impact during challenging times is profound. My journey brought with it overwhelming emotions, a common response that many can relate to. I used positive affirmations for many years to help me overcome these tough times. I would write something positive about myself, for example, "You can do anything you set your mind to," on a sticky note and put it on my bathroom mirror. When I wake up every morning, I am reminded that I can conquer the world. Before you know it, you can have several reaffirming quotes on your bathroom mirror, cheering you on to seize the day. This may seem silly or frivolous, but you will be amazed at how inspirational this will be when you're having a bad day.

Another one of my favorite tools is volunteering. Volunteering has an enormous impact on healing. Serving a cause greater than oneself provides fulfillment and redirects focus positively. It's well-documented that volunteering can diminish stress and elevate mood by stimulating dopamine release, leading to a richer sense of purpose and satisfaction. Plus, it opens avenues to forge new, supportive friendships—essential for emotional support and stress alleviation during healing. By spending time volunteering, you will gain a sense of meaning and appreciation that has a therapeutic quality to it.

Lastly, pursue a passion. There's never been a better moment to engage with what you love. For me, the darkest period led to the discovery and cultivation of my passion for helping others, which became my lifeline. I focused so intently on developing my passion that I began to heal and didn't realize it. I guess you can say it saved me, and now I dedicate my life to saving others. So, dive into your interests. They can rekindle joy and, by filling your life with positivity, leave little space for negativity.

Coping Mechanisms: Battling the Darkness

While each journey through trauma is unique, there are coping mechanisms that will help relieve some of your anxiety. It's okay if you struggle to figure out what skills work. Try all of the coping skills on for size. Finding the strategies that work best for you is essential to the healing process. Here are a few coping strategies that may be beneficial to you in reducing the stress and anxiety that come with trauma:

01. Engaging in Self-Care Activities

Incorporate rest, nutrition, and exercise into your routine to boost physical health and manage anxiety. Adequate rest recharges your mind, proper nutrition supports brain health and mood regulation, and regular exercise stimulates endorphins to uplift your spirits. Prioritizing these self-care practices can diminish anxiety and elevate your life's quality.

02. Seeking Support from Others

Reaching out for support is a courageous step on your healing path. Conversations with trusted friends or family can offer solace and perspective, providing emotional relief. Additionally, therapy with a trauma specialist can impart valuable tools and personalized strategies for anxiety management. Therapy is a secure environment to process emotions, enhance self-awareness, and understand your trauma. Seeking professional assistance is a testament to your dedication to self-care and a healthier future.

03. Practicing Relaxation Techniques

Relaxation methods like deep breathing, meditation, and mindfulness are vital for mental serenity and reducing anxiety. These practices center your awareness on the present, nurturing tranquility. Deep breathing exercises, focusing on the rhythm of your breath, trigger a relaxation response that calms the heart rate and lowers blood pressure. Meditation encourages inner peace by turning attention inward, and regular mindfulness helps you witness thoughts without judgment. Although mastery of these techniques requires practice, they are profoundly rewarding for managing anxiety and fostering well-being.

04. Engaging in Creative Outlets

Creative activities such as writing, painting, or playing music offer a judgment-free zone for self-expression and have therapeutic effects for those dealing with trauma. These outlets provide a unique language for articulating complex emotions and experiences. Writing allows for introspection and self-discovery, painting captures emotional landscapes beyond words, and music creates resonant melodies that can articulate feelings and foster healing. Immersing in these activities can be both comforting and contributory to personal growth and recovery.

05. Give yourself time and patience

Healing is a journey that requires time and patience. It's important to understand that the path to recovery often includes both strides and stumbles. Celebrate every achievement, no matter how minor, as you move toward healing. Embracing this journey helps you persevere through challenges without losing heart. Recognizing every small success is crucial for sustaining motivation and a positive outlook. Each accomplishment, whether a modest advancement or a shift in your emotional state, is praiseworthy. Acknowledging your progress reinforces your confidence and reminds you of the distance you've already covered on your path to recovery.

▌ Suit of Armor: Forging Ahead

With the right tools and resources at your disposal, you are well-equipped to take on the healing process and move forward. It's important to remember that healing is a journey, and it may have its ups and downs. But with determination and the support of these valuable tools, you can navigate through any challenges that come your way. Now is the time to embrace your strength and tenacity. Trust in yourself and believe that you have what it takes to overcome obstacles, heal, and grow from your experiences. Take each day as an opportunity for growth and progress. You're doing an exceptional job building up your war chest of tools; now it's time for action. Forge ahead with confidence, knowing you are equipped with everything you need to navigate this transformative process successfully. Onward toward a brighter future filled with growth, resilience, and inner peace.

Equipped with the right tools, you're ready to engage in the healing process. Healing is indeed a journey, with its share of challenges, but with resilience and these tools at your disposal, you're prepared for the road ahead. Now is the time to harness your strength and resolve. Trust in your ability to surmount obstacles, heal, and grow. Each day is a chance for advancement, and you're doing admirably in gathering your arsenal of resources. Step forward with assurance, armed with the necessities for a successful transformation.

It might seem intimidating to implement these tools; the thought alone can be overwhelming. Challenge yourself to muster the will to embark on this path. All it takes is the first step and the daily commitment to self-motivation. Remember, you're the only one who can walk your path, but you're not alone. I'm here to accompany you, provide guidance and inspiration, and remind you that solitude in your struggle is an illusion. This book aims to illuminate the path to post-traumatic growth and spur you to pursue it. You deserve to advance toward happiness, and I aim to support your ascent.

Obstacles will arise to test your resolve. The key is to learn to navigate the shadows. Resist the seductive whispers of despair and break free from trauma's hold. A life beyond trauma, while frightening, is ripe with opportunity for those who remain focused, resilient, and forgiving and who keep the faith. Challenges are inevitable, but with consistent effort, you can navigate through the darkness toward enlightenment. It is in these moments that you discover a will to heal and start on a path of rebirth and renewal.

So, take this moment to receive the accolades for beginning this healing venture. Recognizing the darkness and seeking the internal light takes true bravery. Your suit of armor—built from your experiences, knowledge, and support—will protect you from further harm. Acknowledge your progress and ensure you're accompanied by those who bolster your healing. Surrounding yourself with individuals who support and uplift you can make a significant difference in your healing process. Together, you can create a positive environment that fosters growth and well-being.

Believe in the power of your inner fortitude as you step onto the path of healing. Trust your instincts to find practices that genuinely speak to you, whether it's therapy, meditation, creative pursuits, or other forms of self-expression. These should serve your unique journey and enrich your soul. The decision to heal is the foundational step; now, continue on with unwavering courage. Growth thrives beyond the familiar, so embrace the new and venture into the unknown with an open heart. Have faith in your abilities, knowing each stride forward is a stride towards your aspirations. You possess the strength to accomplish remarkable feats—maintain that belief as you navigate the rewarding path of self-discovery and development.

The trek through trauma's shadow is arduous but essential. We understand the emotional turmoil post-trauma, the confusion, fear, and sense of loss it can induce. Now, with clear goals and the courage to confront challenges directly, we can pierce through that darkness. We're equipped with coping strategies that fortify our resolve towards post-traumatic growth. As we proceed, we'll delve into how these experiences reshape our beliefs and perspectives. Our convictions and viewpoints sculpt our reality—our thoughts lead to actions, actions to habits, habits to character, and character to destiny.

Perhaps the butterfly is proof that you can go through a great deal of darkness yet become something beautiful.

~ Unknown

CHAPTER 3

Transforming Beliefs and Perspectives

Post Traumatic Growth: Examining the Power of Faith

In the shadowed aftermath of trauma, one crucial element often remains overlooked on our path to recovery: faith. This potent force can lead us to profound healing, transforming our beliefs and perspectives. Faith infuses life with purpose and direction, dispelling doubts and the fear of inevitable misfortune. It nurtures the hope that things will improve, even when solutions seem obscure. Faith fortifies us with the resilience to confront adversity, the valor to surmount barriers, and the serenity to traverse life's fluctuations. Sometimes, faith is the very balm we need to alleviate the wounds inflicted by trauma.

Traumatic events frequently challenge our belief systems, prompting introspection about life's meaning and purpose. Faith can support us in ways beyond the reach of conventional remedies. It is a sanctuary for the soul that helps us find coherence in our suffering and endows us with fortitude amidst strife. Faith is the gentle whisper that reassures us in moments of despair and the unwavering companion that guides us through tumultuous times, even when deliverance seems unattainable. If your faith wavers, remember there are paths to rekindle its flame.

Strengthening our faith to foster post-traumatic growth is a deeply personal journey. The challenge lies in discovering what resonates with your spirit, providing comfort and nourishment for your soul. This self-discovery makes faith more accessible, setting the stage for evolution. Believing in yourself, the healing process and your inherent strength becomes the driving force behind your growth. Embracing vulnerability and lowering your guard creates room for transformation and renewal.

In the throes of uncertainty, faith acts as a sanctuary, offering solace and a promise of hope. It illuminates our path during the darkest times, assuring us of a dawn yet to come. With faith, we find solace in the midst of turmoil, trusting in a greater purpose that steers us toward healing. The potency of faith lies in its capacity to reshape our beliefs, fortify our inner resolve, and catalyze profound change. By harnessing this dynamic, we open ourselves to a world of possibilities for recovery and self-realization.

The Exploration of Thoughts and Beliefs: The Evolution of Change

Trauma can profoundly disrupt our foundational beliefs, shaking our sense of security and trust. This upheaval can lead to a radical shift in how we view ourselves and the world, prompting us to reevaluate our assumptions. Though daunting, this period of questioning is also ripe with potential for growth and self-discovery. It's crucial to recognize that change is an inherent part of healing, guiding us through life's adversities and transitions. Welcoming change is a step toward mastering new coping strategies and establishing a renewed belief system.

Post-trauma, a reassessment of core beliefs and values is common, often leading to self-doubt. This internal conflict, while uncomfortable, also lays the groundwork for fresh perspectives and personal development. It might be instinctive to resist these shifts in viewpoint but accepting them paves the way for significant personal evolution. Acknowledging trauma's influence on our psyche enables us to forge new narratives of strength and endurance. We begin to identify as survivors, not victims, and each stride forward affirms our capacity to prevail against hardships.

To achieve the coveted post-traumatic growth, we must embark on a journey of altering our thought patterns. Cultivating motivational thoughts can catalyze a change in direction, enhancing self-belief and transforming obstacles into opportunities. It's the shift in mindset that can make a world of difference— alter your thoughts, and you alter your reality. The mind's power is formidable; reshaping our thought processes can lead to significant life improvements. Change is an inside job. By harnessing the strength of our thoughts and consciously striving for mental transformation, we lay the foundation for a richer, more rewarding existence. Embrace the process of change deliberately and watch as your life unfolds into new realms of joy and achievement.

The power of thought is more than mere wishful thinking; it's a concept grounded in scientific evidence. Research supports the notion that positive thinking significantly impacts our mental and physical health, reducing stress and enhancing well-being. Repeated thoughts become integral to our identity, shaping our beliefs, emotions, decisions, and actions. These patterns, which only we have the power to alter, are potent tools for transformation, especially during the healing process. Discard negative thoughts to clear the way for new, constructive insights.

Reframing negative thoughts is a pivotal technique for altering your mindset. It makes you more mindful of the link between thoughts, feelings, and behaviors and transforms critical self-talk into empowering affirmations. Distinguishing detrimental thoughts from beneficial ones can help you become flexible in thinking and master your thought processes. This discernment can shift your perspective on any situation, revealing hidden positives and lessons within challenges. Negative thoughts can disrupt daily life and sleep, hindering happiness and health. By purging them, you enable change and growth.

In essence, embracing change is key to becoming the best version of ourselves. Accepting change as a fundamental aspect of life allows us to face it with optimism, unlocking new opportunities. It liberates us from outdated patterns and habits, spurring personal development. This acceptance of change strengthens us, fosters wisdom, and places us at the helm of our life's direction. We are not bound by our past; within us lies the capacity to author a new chapter of our existence. Within each of us lies the power to shape our own destiny and write a new narrative for our lives. By embracing change, learning from experiences, and setting positive intentions, we can author a fresh chapter filled with endless possibilities and potential.

▍ Cognitive Strategies to Evoke Change

The influence our thoughts have on our emotions and actions is astonishing. To initiate change, especially in the aftermath of trauma, it's crucial to shift our mental landscape away from negative patterns. Cognitive strategies offer robust tools for this transformation, targeting the pessimistic thought patterns and beliefs trauma often instills. By embracing these techniques, we learn to question and reshape our thinking, fostering a more affirmative outlook. This cognitive retooling not only deepens our emotional understanding but also cultivates resilient coping skills, empowering us to take command of our lives. Let's delve into these transformative strategies.

Strategy 1: Reframing

Cognitive restructuring, also referred to as reframing, is a powerful technique aimed at transforming your mindset and enhancing your overall well-being. By deliberately confronting and reshaping negative thought patterns, this approach enables you to substitute them with more constructive ones. The process of reframing involves recognizing negative or distorted thinking tendencies, like overgeneralization or catastrophizing, and substituting them with more grounded and rational alternatives. Ultimately, it empowers you to adopt a renewed perspective.

■ **Recognize the Negative Thoughts**

Become aware of and acknowledge negative thought patterns without self-criticism. Understand that these thoughts do not define your character or potential.

■ **Challenge the Negativity**

When a negative thought arises, scrutinize its truth. Assess whether it's based on concrete evidence, mere assumptions, or residual effects from past experiences. This often reveals that many negative thoughts lack a realistic foundation.

■ **Find Alternative Perspectives**

Seek different interpretations for the negative thoughts. Entertain various viewpoints that might cast a more positive light on the situation.

■ **Practice Gratitude**

Cultivate gratitude by focusing on the aspects of your life that you're thankful for. This shifts your focus from negative ruminations to positive acknowledgments.

■ **Replace with Positive Affirmations**

Replace negative thoughts with affirmative statements. Regular repetition of these affirmations can firmly embed them in your thought process.

■ **Surround Yourself with Positivity**

Encircle yourself with positive influences that bolster your reframing efforts. This could be uplifting literature, podcasts, or relationships that nurture a constructive mindset.

Strategy 2: Though Stopping

The "Thought Stopping" technique serves as a pivotal method for breaking free from negative thought patterns. When you catch yourself dwelling on negativity, swiftly halt the thought and redirect your focus to something positive. This cognitive strategy plays a crucial role in steering your mindset towards one that is optimistic and conducive to productivity. By intercepting negative thoughts upon their emergence, you assert control over your cognitive processes. This proactive approach empowers you to confront and replace detrimental thoughts with uplifting ones, thereby averting the downward spiral of self-doubt and pessimism. Remember, mastering control over your thoughts is paramount for instigating meaningful change. Through the deliberate cessation of negative thoughts, coupled with the practice of mindfulness, you cultivate a positive mindset conducive to achieving your aspirations.

- **Notice the thought**
    - Example: "I will never get over what happened to me."

- **Stop the thought**
    - Example: Say "Stop" or envision something that represents the stop.

- **Reroute your mind to an inspiring or distracting thought**
    - Words of encouragement, empowering memory, listening to music

This method has had a profound impact on my life. Initially, I employed a simple yet effective approach to intercepting my negative thoughts—I used a rubber band. I placed an ordinary rubber band around my wrist, and whenever a negative thought surfaced, I would snap the rubber band with gentle force. This action served as a distraction, allowing me to redirect my focus towards something uplifting. Over time, I developed the ability to halt intrusive thoughts independently, which has been incredibly empowering.

Strategy 3: Replacing Negative Thoughts with Crafted Positive Affirmations

The concept behind this strategy is straightforward: replace negative thoughts with personally crafted positive affirmations. To implement this technique, identify the negative thoughts that hinder your progress and develop affirmations that directly challenge them. For instance, if you frequently think, "I'm not good enough," counteract this with an affirmation like "I am capable and deserving of success." Regularly repeating these affirmations helps rewire your brain and shift your mindset towards more empowering thoughts. Consistent reinforcement of positive self-talk lays the groundwork for change, fostering a confident and optimistic outlook over time. As these affirmations become ingrained in your thinking, they shape your perception of yourself and your approach to challenges.

An illustrative example is the case of Jania, an 11-year-old client who sought treatment following the loss of her parents. Initially struggling to cope with her grief, Jania eventually began to make progress with therapeutic intervention. However, her sense of inadequacy and unworthiness intensified due to the absence of parental support. Upon exploring various coping strategies, Jania found resonance in crafting her own positive affirmations. Transitioning from beliefs of incapacity to affirmations like "I am a reflection of my parents, and I will make them proud," she embarked on a journey of self-affirmation. Through consistent reflection and practice, Jania blossomed, embracing the belief that she was destined for success to honor her parents' legacy. Her transformation serves as a compelling testament to the transformative power of positive affirmations— what we speak into the universe manifests into reality.

▌ Strengthening your Path to Change

Embarking on the journey to transform your beliefs, thoughts, and actions necessitates surrounding yourself with a supportive network of individuals. These allies offer encouragement, guidance, and a sympathetic ear when necessary. By connecting with like-minded individuals, you fortify your support network, seeking out those who share your aspirations and values. Such companions are better positioned to comprehend your journey and offer invaluable insights. Engage with relevant groups or communities, and participate in self-help meetings, both online and locally, to foster connections with others on a similar path. These engagements serve as wellsprings of knowledge and inspiration.

While the journey to revamp our beliefs, thoughts, and actions may pose challenges, the rewards are immense. Committing to this transformative process unlocks our full potential and enables us to surmount limitations. Practice patience with yourself, cultivate a robust support network, and regularly assess your progress. By focusing on altering these facets of your life, you equip yourself to confront challenges, seize opportunities, and effect lasting, positive change. By honing in on refining these aspects of your life, you empower yourself to tackle obstacles head-on, capitalize on advantageous situations, and enact enduring, beneficial transformations. This intentional focus serves as a catalyst for personal growth in the face of life's uncertainties.

We take an active stance in our healing journey by empowering ourselves with cognitive strategies. Through reframing experiences, cultivating mindfulness in daily life, and challenging unproductive thought patterns, we break free from the constraints hindering our progress. While navigating the aftermath of trauma, it's essential to acknowledge that the journey of overcoming trauma is unique to each individual. Seek professional assistance if necessary and surround yourself with individuals who comprehend your journey and provide unwavering support. With time, patience, and the arsenal of cognitive strategies at your disposal, you can empower yourself to heal and thrive beyond trauma.

▮ Refocusing your energy

By embarking on a journey of self-discovery and healing, you can reignite your inner spark and discover the transformative power of post-traumatic growth. Your journey revolves around refocusing your energy, revitalizing your spirit, and unlocking the potential for restoration. It's natural to feel drained as if your zest for life has waned in the wake of trauma. You might even believe that your life has been irreparably altered by past events. But let me reassure you: that's simply not true. In fact, it's quite the opposite.

The root of our suffering often lies in our relentless focus on past trauma, causing us to overlook the abundance of positives in our lives. Our brains are wired to keep us safe by constantly reminding us of past dangers, but this perpetual vigilance can hinder our ability to move forward. It's crucial to give ourselves the space to break free from this cycle of rumination and allow ourselves to grow. The idea is to give yourself permission to let go of what no longer serves you and create space for new beginnings. It is not until then that we can place ourselves in a space to see what lies ahead.

The solution lies in redirecting our energy towards positive endeavors, effectively signaling to our brains that we are safe and capable of thriving. To replenish your energy after trauma, prioritize self-care and engage in activities that promote healing. This may involve seeking support from loved ones or professional counselors who can provide guidance and understanding. Remember, renewing your energy is an ongoing process that requires dedication and perseverance. By embracing the journey of post-traumatic growth and actively pursuing opportunities for self-renewal, you will gradually reclaim your vitality and flourish beyond your wildest expectations.

To rejuvenate and encourage post-traumatic growth, it's crucial to adopt self-care routines that enhance your well-being. This can involve meditative practices, consistent exercise, and ensuring ample rest. Diving into creative activities, such as painting, writing, dancing, or playing an instrument, can also be profoundly therapeutic. These outlets not only allow for emotional expression but also help you access your innate resilience. It's vital to approach this regenerative process with kindness towards yourself, allowing healing to unfold at a pace that feels right for you. Embracing this journey will enable you to recover your vitality and pave the way for a life marked by resilience and optimism.

Refocusing your energy is about making mindful choices in how you allocate your time and efforts. Evaluating your priorities helps pinpoint aspects of your life that may be sapping your energy, such as detrimental relationships or unproductive routines. By identifying and eliminating these drains, you're empowered to make deliberate choices, steering your focus towards uplifting activities and relationships. Refocusing also involves setting clear objectives and ensuring your actions are in harmony with these aims. Streamlining your commitments to align with your personal growth and well-being creates room for enriching experiences and self-fulfillment. Refocusing isn't about increasing your activities—it's about enhancing the quality of what you do. It's about caring for yourself, cherishing valuable relationships, embracing your passions, and dedicating yourself to personal growth. By thoughtfully directing your time and efforts, you regain command of your life, fostering a deeper sense of purpose and contentment.

So, pause to consider how you're distributing your energy. Could it be better utilized? Decide today to concentrate on what's genuinely significant to you. Wise energy investment is key to unlocking our utmost potential for achievement and joy. Prioritize what truly matters to you and make a conscious choice today to direct your energy towards meaningful and fulfilling pursuits.

Exploring the Roles of Spirituality and Existential Growth

Trauma has an unparalleled ability to shake us to our core, leaving us grappling with existential questions and a sense of profound uncertainty. However, amidst the chaos, there lies an opportunity for profound healing and transformation through the exploration of spirituality and existential growth. These dimensions of personal development are especially pertinent in the aftermath of trauma, offering pathways to meaning-making and resilience. Exploring these roles opens up a world of possibilities when searching for a way out of the darkness.

For me, spirituality serves as a guiding light, illuminating the path toward transcendence and connection with the profound mysteries of existence. It provides a framework for understanding life beyond its material manifestations, offering solace and reassurance in times of adversity. Whether through a connection with a higher power or a sense of communion with the universe, spirituality offers a source of comfort and wisdom that transcends individual suffering. It's the invisible blanket hugging you when you need it most allowing comfort and solace.

In parallel, existential growth beckons us to embark on a journey of self-discovery and introspection. It invites us to confront our deepest beliefs and values, grapple with existential dilemmas, and unearth meaning amidst life's inherent challenges. Through this process of exploration and reflection, we glean insights into our own existence and find purpose in our suffering. By courageously confronting and processing our traumas, we not only transcend their grip but also emerge from the crucible of adversity stronger and more resilient than before. I often view this as the butterfly emerging from its cocoon only to be transformed into something more vibrant, beautiful and unique.

Embracing spirituality and embarking on existential exploration are transformative acts of self-care and empowerment. These practices facilitate healing from past wounds while nurturing a profound sense of compassion and empathy for others who have traversed similar paths. As we delve into the depths of our spiritual and existential landscapes, we unearth reservoirs of resilience and wisdom that enable us to navigate life's complexities with grace and fortitude. It is this foothold that can catapult us into the next phase of our growth potential.

Spirituality and Existential Growth: Wading in Unfamiliar Territory

The profound link between spirituality and existential growth may seem unfamiliar to some, but that's perfectly alright. This journey isn't about conforming to any specific religious doctrine or philosophical ideology. Instead, it's a deeply personal voyage that urges individuals to tap into their inner wisdom and intuition, irrespective of their spiritual leanings. Through this wisdom one can discover a deeper meaning to who they are and what they desire to become. This thirst for gaining a clearer understanding evolves into a portal between being stuck in your trauma and emotional healing

For those starting without a robust spiritual foundation, the journey commences with nurturing self-awareness and fostering an open mindset. It involves exploring a plethora of philosophies, teachings, and practices that resonate with one's unique values and experiences. There's no one-size-fits-all approach here; each person's path is shaped by their own circumstances and aspirations. By embracing curiosity, engaging in introspection, and remaining receptive to new perspectives, profound insights are unearthed, and tranquility is found amidst the pursuit of post-traumatic growth.

While some may find solace in traditional religious practices, others may seek enlightenment through alternative avenues. The beauty of personal growth lies in its adaptability. We possess the freedom to carve out our own distinct path toward healing, guided solely by what feels authentic and meaningful to us individually. Embracing the autonomy to decide our own unique path toward personal growth grants us the opportunity to strive for the sought-after emotional metamorphosis we all hope to experience.

As we traverse the terrain of post-traumatic growth, let's not underestimate the power of faith. It serves as a beacon of solace, hope, and resilience during the darkest of times, instilling in us a belief in something greater than ourselves and providing direction when the path seems obscured. Additionally, it's crucial to recognize that our beliefs and thoughts deeply influence our progress along this journey. Incorporating cognitive strategies can offer clarity of mind, enabling us to gain fresh perspectives and embrace concepts like spirituality and existential growth.

Incorporating these concepts adds depth to our healing journey, guiding us toward a clearer understanding of how to channel our energy toward positive change. By actively pursuing this transformation, we foster an environment conducive to growth and cultivate inner resilience. It's through this intentional journey that we embrace personal transformation and embark on a path of self-discovery and empowerment.

Trauma creates change you don't choose. Healing is about creating the change you choose.

~Michelle Rosenthal

CHAPTER 4

Cultivating Growth and Strength

Internal and External Resources: Contributions to Growth

As we embark on the next leg of our healing journey, let's delve into the invaluable contributions of internal and external resources in guiding our path. Building upon the groundwork laid in the preceding chapters, we continue our exploration of the multifaceted impact of trauma and the avenues for restoration. Incorporating internal and external resources helps to fortify our resolve and strengthen our desire for growth.

In our previous discussions, we illuminated the profound ways in which trauma disrupts our lives, leaving us feeling adrift and disempowered. Yet, amidst the chaos, a plethora of resources beckoned to assist us in reclaiming a semblance of control. It's essential to recognize the pivotal role played by both internal and external resources in fostering post-traumatic growth.

The first step towards harnessing these resources lies in acknowledging the shifts that have occurred in our daily lives since the experience of trauma. By introspecting on these changes, we gain insight into the areas where support and intervention are most needed. For instance, if a fear of loud noises once startles us but has then subsides, it behooves us to recognize the stimuli behind this change, thereby paving the way for targeted solutions.

Trauma often engenders a sense of isolation, prompting us to seek solace in the embrace of our familial and social circles. While these relationships offer invaluable external support, it's not uncommon to encounter barriers to effective communication and understanding. Our loved ones may falter in providing the support we seek, either due to a lack of comprehension or an inability to articulate their assistance. However, beneath this surface lies the potential for profound connection and guidance. Our families may hold the keys to unlocking the resources essential for our recovery. They may illuminate pathways to healing, lending a helping hand in our quest for restoration. While they may not fully comprehend our experiences, their unwavering support serves as a beacon of strength and solidarity.

It's crucial to approach discussions about the traumatic incident with a sense of preparedness for potential reactions from friends or family members. It's not uncommon for individuals affected by trauma to react defensively when confronted with their actions during or after the event. This may lead to feelings of anger or blame, but it's essential to recognize that their intent isn't to assign fault. Rather, they're seeking understanding regarding your behavior and exploring possibilities for different outcomes. In such situations, patience and openness are key virtues, paving the way for meaningful dialogue and mutual comprehension.

Conversations serve as catalysts for healing and offer opportunities for transformative growth in the aftermath of trauma. They provide a platform to process emotions, gain new perspectives, and work through the lingering effects of the event. As we articulate our thoughts and experiences, we gain clarity and begin to release ourselves from the grip of trauma. The act of speaking out is a potent instrument on our journey toward healing, allowing us to reclaim our identity as survivors rather than victims. Though discussing traumatic experiences may be triggering, it's through these conversations that we find the strength to move forward and embrace a renewed outlook on life.

With an understanding of external resources in mind, let's now delve into harnessing our internal reservoirs of strength. Among these internal resources lies the inherent resilience and fortitude within each of us. While it's natural to focus on the gravity of the trauma and its impact, it's equally important to recognize and celebrate our inner strength. Amidst adversity, we often discover depths of resilience we never knew existed. Acknowledging this reservoir of strength offers a positive focal point during challenging times, empowering us to navigate through adversity with renewed determination.

Often, we underestimate the wealth of resources nestled within us. awaiting activation to aid in our healing journey. Below are some internal reservoirs you might consider harnessing as you navigate the path to healing. By tapping into your inner strength and resilience, you can unlock these invaluable assets that lie dormant within you:

■ Self-Compassion:

Direct your focus toward extending kindness and gentleness to yourself. Remain attuned to your thoughts and emotions, offering yourself the same compassion you would readily extend to a friend facing similar circumstances.

■ Gratitude:

Cultivate a sense of gratitude for the blessings present in your life at this moment. Embracing gratitude amidst adversity fosters inner peace and tranquility, serving as a steadfast anchor amid life's storms.

■ Self-Soothing Strategies:

Explore practices such as meditation or yoga to cultivate relaxation and alleviate stress. These activities empower your body to remain composed in the face of adversity, fostering a sense of calmness and enhancing your overall mood.

Our minds and bodies harbor remarkable capabilities that stand ready to accompany us on our journey toward healing. By nurturing these internal resources, we empower ourselves to traverse through challenges with resilience and grace, embarking on a transformative path toward wholeness and restoration. Allowing these nuances into our fragmented lives serves as the adhesive to put us back together again.

Implementing these internal resources into your daily life is simpler than you might think. They serve as comforting pillars and outlets for fostering healing and personal growth. With dedication and a commitment to achieving post-traumatic growth, you'll uncover a solid framework that propels you toward success. Grant yourself the grace and space needed to identify activities and resources that resonate with you. Once established and integrated into your routine, you'll find yourself on a transformative journey, emerging as a resilient and self-assured individual, liberated from the chains of trauma.

Consider the experience of Wesley, a former client of mine, who discovered profound support through an unexpected avenue. Initially reluctant to leave the confines of his apartment, Wesley heeded advice to explore hobbies or activities for relief. Despite initial struggles, he ventured to a neighborhood fitness center and reluctantly participated in classes offered. To his surprise, he found solace and renewal in a yoga class, describing it as a sanctuary to unburden his mind and rejuvenate his spirit. Over time, Wesley's passion for yoga blossomed, leading him to become a yoga instructor for a nonprofit support group. What began as a leap of faith evolved into a transformative journey of self-discovery and empowerment, showcasing the remarkable potency of internal resources when embraced wholeheartedly.

▎ The Next Level: Identify Ways to Elevate Yourself

In the aftermath of trauma, navigating the path towards healing and growth may seem off-putting, yet there are simple, impactful steps you can take to uplift yourself and propel forward:

- **Grant Yourself Permission to Feel:**

Acknowledge and embrace your emotions without judgment or suppression. Permit yourself to experience the full spectrum of feelings, recognizing that it's a natural and necessary part of the healing process. With practice, this becomes a powerful tool for self-awareness and resilience.

- **Prioritize Physical Self-Care:**

Nurture your physical well-being by adopting habits that promote vitality and resilience. Ensure adequate nutrition, rest, and exercise to support your body's healing process. Additionally, avoid isolation and prioritize exposure to natural elements like sunlight and fresh air, which play pivotal roles in rejuvenation and restoration.

- **Seek Support and Connection:**

Don't hesitate to reach out for assistance when needed. Connect with friends who offer compassionate support and understanding, creating a nurturing environment for healing. Similarly, engage with family members who may not fully comprehend your experience but are willing to lend a listening ear. Embracing vulnerability and fostering meaningful connections serves as a catalyst for growth, propelling you toward the next stage of post-traumatic evolution.

When it comes to bouncing back from trauma, it's not just about survival; it's about thriving. It's about reclaiming your power and rediscovering the joy that life has to offer. Here are some strategies to elevate yourself and embrace the journey of healing:

- **Embrace What Lifts Your Spirit:**

Dive into activities that ignite your passion and bring a smile to your face. Whether it's sweating it out in a workout session, losing yourself in the pages of a captivating book, or experimenting with a new recipe in the kitchen, indulge in what makes your heart sing. These moments of joy are like beacons of light guiding you through the darkest of times.

- **Shift Your Focus to Gratitude:**

In the midst of pain, it's easy to overlook the blessings in our lives. Take a moment each day to count your blessings and jot them down in a gratitude journal. Remind yourself of the small victories, the moments of kindness, and the sparks of joy that still exist amidst the chaos. Cultivating an attitude of gratitude can work wonders in shifting your perspective and lifting your spirits.

- **Explore Uncharted Territories:**

Step outside your comfort zone and explore new avenues for healing and growth. For me, joining a women's tackle football team was a game-changer. It pushed me to my limits, challenged me both mentally and physically, and provided a sense of camaraderie that I had been craving. Find what lights a fire within you and pursue it with enthusiasm. You never know where it might lead.

- **Carve Out Moments for Reflection:**

Amidst the hustle and bustle of life, carve out quiet moments for self-reflection. Take stock of how far you've come, acknowledge your resilience, and celebrate your victories, no matter how small. Setting aside time for introspection allows you to reconnect with yourself and chart a course for the future with clarity and purpose.

- **Reward Yourself for Progress:**

Every step forward, no matter how small, deserves recognition. Set achievable goals for yourself and celebrate each milestone along the way. Treat yourself to something special—a bubble bath, a delicious meal, or a cozy movie night. You're putting in the work, so don't forget to acknowledge and honor your efforts.

Remember, healing is a journey, not a destination. Be patient with yourself, be kind to yourself, and above all, believe in yourself. You are stronger than you know, and brighter days are ahead.

▌ The Rebirth: Redefining Courage and Motivation

Courage and motivation—two pillars that define our capacity to face life's challenges head-on. Yet, their presence in our lives is often a matter of perception. Courage, as defined, is the ability to confront something that instills fear within us. It's about pushing past our apprehensions, despite the uncertainties that lie ahead. But how do we recognize this elusive quality within ourselves? How do we truly understand and embrace our own brand of courage?

Firstly, it's crucial to acknowledge that courage comes in various forms, each unique to the individual. For some, courage may manifest as a bold confrontation of fears, while for others, it may be found in the quiet strength to admit vulnerability and seek support. It's not about conforming to a single definition but rather about discovering what resonates most authentically with your essence.

Take a moment to reflect on your own understanding of courage. What actions or qualities do you associate with courage? Is it the unwavering determination to face adversity alone, or is it the humility to admit when you need a helping hand? There's no one-size-fits-all answer. True courage is deeply personal—it's about aligning with your inner truth and embracing the courage that feels most genuine to you.

Courage isn't about being fearless; it's about acknowledging your fears and moving forward in spite of them. It's about honoring your vulnerabilities and recognizing them as sources of strength rather than weaknesses. By embracing your unique definition of courage, you empower yourself to navigate life's challenges with resilience and authenticity.

So, as you embark on this journey of self-discovery, remember that courage is not a destination but a continuous evolution—a journey of growth and empowerment. Embrace your fears, embrace your vulnerabilities, and above all, embrace the courage that resides within you. This newly defined courage is your chariot ready to whisk you off into a life filled with hope, recovery and prosperity.

Motivation—the driving force behind our actions, the spark that propels us toward our goals. It's not something we acquire from external sources; rather, it's an internal state of mind that fuels our aspirations and endeavors. But what happens when trauma strikes and our motivation wanes? How do we reignite that inner fire and reclaim our sense of purpose? How do we convince ourselves that we can make it through the other side of this journey?

First and foremost, it's essential to reconnect with what truly motivates you. Dive deep into your inner landscape and ask yourself: What brings me joy? What fills me with energy and enthusiasm? Identifying these sources of intrinsic motivation lays the foundation for regaining your sense of purpose. Once you've pinpointed what drives you, it's time to forge the connection between these passions and your life goals. How do your core motivators align with the aspirations you hold dear? Recognizing this link is pivotal in channeling your energy toward meaningful endeavors.

Finally, consider how leveraging your motivations can propel you toward your objectives. How can these sources of inspiration make your journey smoother and more fulfilling? By harnessing the power of your inner drive, you empower yourself to overcome obstacles and achieve your aspirations. You fuel your deepest desires with purpose and enthusiasm making them both attainable and real.

Remember, motivation isn't just about pushing forward; it's about embracing the journey with purpose and determination. By understanding what motivates you and channeling it positively, you pave the way for profound personal growth and transformation. Embrace this shift in perspective as a catalyst for unlocking your full potential and embracing a renewed sense of purpose.

I've touched on the concept of post-traumatic growth, which is about making sense of our struggles, channeling pain into empowerment, and transforming setbacks into advances. It's taking risks, learning from missteps, and asking for help when it's most critical. It's about recovering our footing after numerous stumbles, allowing ourselves to be open, and maintaining self-belief even when we feel alone. Post-traumatic growth is not a myth; it's a reality that occurs globally every day and is waiting to unfold in your life too. The capacity to rediscover motivation and courage following trauma lies in seeing the world as an expanse of opportunities and prospects, not as a source of dread.

It's vital to acknowledge that the trauma you've encountered is not your fault, and neither is any delay in addressing it; such is the nature of trauma. Each person's response to it is unique. What counts is the distance you've navigated on the path to recovery and the healing you're destined to realize. You might face hurdles, yet each obstacle is a steppingstone for further growth. Whatever the future holds, this growth will endow you with strength beyond your imagination. Trust in your talents, your dreams, your aspirations, and your objectives. This trust is the catalyst that will propel you into an odyssey of transformation and new beginnings.

Breakthrough: Rebuilding Emotional Strength

Enduring tough times can take a toll, yet here you are, ready to fortify your emotional resilience. It's about learning to tackle stress effectively, preventing it from becoming overwhelming or causing lasting harm. Plus, it's about nurturing strategies to uplift yourself amidst negative emotions. Remember, practical tools exist to help steer you back to a joyful, healthy existence. I'm here to guide you to some of these tools.

When you're faced with an emotional whirlwind and are unsure how to proceed, try the following steps:

1. Inhale deeply and pause before reacting. Giving yourself this space allows your mind to process the event and formulate a fitting response.

2. Assure yourself that the situation, however intense, will pass in time, which can significantly lessen the immediate stress you feel.

Let's explore further what it means to possess emotional strength. This strength is an internal fortress, a deep-seated resilience that we all carry within. It is our inner strength, the skill to harness our mental and physical capabilities to turn dreams into reality. This strength isn't a rare gift bestowed upon a fortunate few; it's a universal potential that anyone can access and develop, regardless of their history or background. Believing in our inner strength is believing in our ability to influence the world around us. To effect such change, we must arm ourselves with knowledge and apply it with deliberate intention in our daily lives, nurturing our existential growth.

Now, as we understand emotional strength better, let's consider some tools to bolster it on your path to recovery:

- Define what you desire and courageously chase after it. It might feel intimidating, or perhaps it seems unattainable, but start by cataloging the things that uplift you—no matter how trivial or grand—and persistently strive to attain them. This process is more than just goal setting; it's a path to heightened self-worth and robust resilience, enabling you to recover more swiftly from future adversities.

- Practice emotional regulation. It's about learning to govern your emotions rather than being governed by them. When waves of anger or sorrow hit, search for the things that restore your equilibrium, be it through music, film, or any other activity that brings solace.

- Pinpoint your emotional triggers. Understanding what unsettles you or sparks discomfort is a strategy for building emotional strength. Recognizing these triggers allows you to prepare for or avoid situations that may throw you off balance in the future.

Reconstructing emotional fortitude in the wake of trauma is a journey, not an instantaneous remedy. It's a path you need not walk alone. This path involves nurturing healthy habits and self-care rituals such as exercise, mindfulness, journaling, or channeling feelings through artistic activities like painting or playing music. Initially, these practices serve as a refuge from inner turmoil, but over time, they can significantly reduce or even heal the anguish. Acknowledging that true growth is an internal process is critical. By engaging in these restorative practices, you cultivate self-kindness and unveil paths to personal enlightenment. By leveraging our innate strengths and focusing on deliberate recovery, we uncover profound significance and purpose in our lives post-trauma.

Cultivating robust coping strategies is crucial in the phase of post-traumatic growth, rebuilding the emotional framework we rely on. These strategies are not just about managing the aftermath; they're about reassembling our emotional architecture. Self-care practices, nurturing a network of support, and engaging in meaningful activities act as cornerstones in this reconstruction. As we face the repercussions of trauma, these elements guide us, promoting healing and personal advancement.

We possess the resilience to transcend adversity and restore our emotional vigor. This requires faith in ourselves, the courage to seek help, and the willingness to tap into our transformative potential. As you forge ahead on this valiant journey towards recovery, remember that trauma, though it scars, does not define us. Our response to it sculpts our identity. Taking the reins of your future, you will reclaim a renewed emotional strength.

▌ Testimony: Winning the War

Ultimately, it's not the events that befall us that define our stories; it's the steps we take in their aftermath. We each carry a tapestry of scars—some still tender, some we'll bear forever. Yet, we aren't etched by these marks. They serve instead as milestones, reminders of the journey we've negotiated and the distances we're yet to conquer. Daily, individuals climb emotional turmoil, healing from yesteryears by crafting new ways to reconcile with memories and forge ahead in life. This collection brims with accounts of resilience, of souls who've tapped into their core fortitude to triumph over life's upheavals. It's my hope that these narratives embolden you as well.

In my own tale, I navigated life's maze with missteps galore, harboring a disdain for not just the world but, most pivotally, myself. The saga of my trauma, a marathon spanning six tumultuous years, forged an armor around my spirit, alienating me from society and the embrace of self-compassion. Shackled by self-revulsion, I deemed myself undeserving of joy. I sought validation and belonging in corners and amongst souls I'd now never imagined approaching. Adrift in an ocean of turbulent emotions, I was void of the means to articulate my chaos or to piece myself back together.

I remember a day when a sudden trigger sent waves of my past traumas crashing over me. It was a familiar, unwelcome sensation, one I had grown weary of. On that day, I vowed to pivot my thoughts elsewhere each time the echoes of my past resurfaced. The challenge was intimidating initially, but persistence reminded me of a strategy I had picked up early in my healing journey. Remember the rubber band I spoke of in an earlier chapter, I wore that rubber band around my wrist, and with every intrusive thought, I'd pull and release it—it reverberated a sharp snap to the skin that jolted me back to the present, allowing room for positivity to enter. This technique is known as thought-stopping. Its impact was transformative; gradually, I learned to replace the old, haunting thoughts with hopeful, affirming ones. My worldview began to shift, and so did my sense of self.

Gaining mastery over these intrusive thoughts brought immense relief. Previously, they would set off a cascade of distress and self-destructive actions, but now I hold the reins. My mind became a sanctuary of clarity. Integrating practices like journaling and daily affirmations was a gradual process, yet the transformation was visible. A newfound self-perception ignited a boost in self-esteem, and small goals set the stage for greater achievements. A new day was breaking, and with it, my drive to evolve blossomed.

Embracing the fresh start before me, I recognized the necessity of a monumental step to realize my post-traumatic growth fully. It was an action I had never envisioned possible, nor had I ever planned to take—it was the act of forgiveness. Though not outlined in my healing strategy, it became evident that it was a critical step; this was the advice I had given my clients. The struggle with the concept lingered for months until one day, the words spontaneously emerged from my mouth when I was confronted with my perpetrator: "I forgive you." In that instant, an immense burden lifted, and I felt an unprecedented lightness. With forgiveness came permission to move forward, though not to forget. Remembering the pain became the driving force behind my purpose today.

Now, life moves as if on autopilot. Each day, I strive for self-improvement and embrace vulnerability once more. My narrative has transformed into a beacon of hope that I share at every opportunity. Once shrouded in shame, my past tribulations now serve as my source of strength. The expedition through post-traumatic growth was prolonged, but my resolve never wavered. The turning point came with the realization that I was exhausted from being dictated by my past emotions. I yearned to liberate the individual entwined with trauma and nurture her evolution into the woman I stand as today. Despite a path tainted by obstacles, my persistence never faltered. I nourished my spirit with optimism and fortified my emotional resilience with faith until I believed I could conquer anything. The transformation has been profound: from a state of fragility and self-loathing to one of strength, confidence, and deep self-love.

It's time to cast off the shackles of trauma and step beyond our scars. There's no singular path to posttraumatic growth; it's a personal expedition that begins wherever you feel most at ease. Apply these tools in the sequence that resonates with you, shaping a journey that's distinctly yours. This is your moment; seize it. Approach it with patience and maintain consistency, for there's nothing beyond your reach. The motivation for change resides within you; set it free.

Your trauma is not your fault, but
healing is your responsibility.

– Unknown

CHAPTER 5

The Power of Forgiveness: Healing, Growth & Personal Freedom

▌ Owning Your Truth: Acknowledgement

The scars of trauma, both seen and unseen, shape our beliefs, behaviors, and the fabric of our relationships, often without our conscious recognition. It is in the act of acknowledging our trauma that we reclaim the helm of our life's journey. The tendency to suppress our experiences, to bury our emotions in the depths of our being, is a common defense mechanism. Yet, confronting our past and embracing the full extent of our pain is the gateway to profound healing and transformation. This acknowledgment is a validation of our experiences, an invitation to mourn, and the first step in unraveling the layers of accumulated hurt.

In the quietness of our pain, we find a crucible for self-reflection and introspection, allowing us to examine the impact of our experiences and identify the patterns and triggers that may inhibit our progress. This confrontation shatters the chains of avoidance and denial. Facing our sorrow directly, we harness the power to govern our emotions, rather than remain their subject. This act of courage, acknowledging our past, is a tribute to our truth and a reclamation of our intrinsic power. It enables us to approach vulnerability as a strength and to utilize our history not as a definition but as a springboard for transformation. By facing our pain unflinchingly, we unlock the doors to healing, resilience, and the dawn of new possibilities.

Striving for rebirth in the aftermath of trauma isn't about denying the events of our past; it's about embracing them as integral threads in the fabric of our life's journey. Acceptance isn't a sign of defeat but a testament to our enduring spirit. This acknowledgment doesn't bind us to our past; it frees us, opening doors to fresh starts and new chapters. Each experience has been a crucial stitch in the tapestry of your resilience. Hold your narrative high, a beacon of courage and hope, for within it lies the keys to boundless opportunities for a rich and rewarding life ahead.

My own acceptance didn't arrive swiftly; it was a gradual ascent over years of self-reflection. What once enshrouded me in shame transformed into a cloak of healing—a testament to my survival. Through my trials, I discovered strength, wisdom, and an indomitable force within. These gifts, born from my struggles, are what I carry forward. The burdensome shadows of trauma? Those I leave behind. Now, my story serves as a torch for those wandering in the dark, a tale not of shame but of pride, marking the path to healing and empowerment.

It takes immense bravery to stand in your truth, to see trauma not as a mark of identity but as a milestone of growth. By reorienting your perspective, you can transmute pain into wisdom and heartache into strength. Your trials, when wielded as instruments of self-evolution, can sculpt you into an unshakeable force. Focus on the virtues carved from your challenges—they are your triumphs, your proofs of a life reshaped by will and grace. As you discard the remnants of negativity, you liberate yourself, stepping lighter on the path of self-discovery. Remember, it is through our most strenuous tests that we unearth our true might. Your journey of healing is not just a solitary quest; it's a narrative to share, a guiding light to others, and a continuous voyage towards becoming the fullest expression of yourself.

Not If but When

Forgiveness wields a transformative power, essential not just for healing from the wounds others have inflicted, but also for the ones we've self-imposed. The act of forgiveness calls for a profound acknowledgment: the trauma we've endured is not our own doing. The journey to forgive my perpetrator was perhaps the most grueling of all my challenges. It seemed an insurmountable task. Yet, as I navigated through the process, seeking solace and strength in my faith, the final piece fell into place—it was forgiveness that would unlock my chains.

Forgiving is not an act of erasure; it doesn't undo the past. Instead, it liberates us from the shackles of negative emotions that once held dominion over our hearts and minds. Clinging to feelings of anger, resentment, and bitterness only nurtures our own agony. I stand before you, a testament to this truth, not from a pedestal, but as someone who has walked the harrowing path you tread. The path to forgiveness isn't about exoneration or amnesia. It's about emancipating oneself from the burdensome weight of grudges that stifle our spirit.

By choosing to forgive, we give ourselves the grace to shed these bonds and step into a new chapter of life. The pain, if we let it, can consume our every thought, sapping the vitality we might otherwise channel into joyous engagement with the world. In forgiveness, there is a release, a freeing of space within us that was once occupied by darkness, now ready to be filled with light, growth, and genuine contentment. It's a reclamation of emotional sovereignty, ensuring that the deeds of another no longer define our state of being. This empowerment is a gateway to breaking the relentless cycle of hurt, opening us to a horizon of tranquility and satisfaction.

Additionally, forgiveness nourishes healthier relationships. It can mend fractured ties and bolster connections weakened by conflicts or misunderstandings. When we extend forgiveness, we embody empathy and set a precedent of kindness that can catalyze positive shifts within us and others. More than an olive branch to those who've wronged us, forgiveness is an act of self-care—a healing balm for wounds that have tethered us to the past, clearing a path for growth and liberation in every facet of life.

Embracing forgiveness is a courageous act, a deliberate choice of compassion over lingering bitterness. This choice is the first step on a transformative journey that replenishes the mind, body, and soul. Though it may be challenging to initiate, this passage toward forgiveness is crucial for our inner peace. It's about valuing our emotional health above the grip of bygone grievances. Clutching onto past hurts immerses us in perpetual unrest while releasing them invites joy and serenity back into our being. Without letting go, we block the inflow of prosperity and joy that awaits us.

Forgiveness is an intimate and individualized voyage, without a prescribed timeframe or roadmap. The process of heartfelt forgiveness can be lengthy, but it is within reach. Our narratives of forgiveness are as diverse as we are, and for some, the depths of past hurts may mean a lifetime's journey of healing. It necessitates introspection, empathy, and a gentle approach towards ourselves and others. By accepting forgiveness, we unlock the doors to emotional maturity and serenity. Trust in your own pace on this healing path, respecting your emotions while keeping your heart open to the possibility of forgiving in your own time. The real question isn't "Will I ever forgive?" but "How do I cultivate the strength to forgive?"

"And forgive us our trespasses.
As we forgive those who trespass against us".

~ Jesus

Finding Inner Peace

The aftermath of trauma can often leave us fragmented and adrift, struggling to comprehend the events that unfolded. Yet, it is in the embrace of our vulnerability that we carve out a sanctuary for understanding and navigating the tumultuous emotions tied to our trauma. This journey into self-awareness helps us reconstruct our shattered selves, discover significance in our trials, and edge closer to a place of tranquility within. Vulnerability also acts as a bridge to others, connecting us with kindred spirits whose shared experiences offer validation and reinforce our resolve to heal. As we venture beyond the trauma, the daunting path becomes one of active engagement in our own narrative, where forgiveness extends inward as much as it does to others.

Self-forgiveness is just as liberating as forgiving those who have wronged us. Too often, we become ensnared in self-reproach, burdening ourselves with misplaced blame. Recognizing that vulnerability is inherent to the human condition—and not a failing—is vital. It is a testament to our strength, not a hallmark of weakness, and acknowledging this can be the first step towards healing. Letting go of self-blame liberates us from the past and ushers in an era of growth, empathy, and self-acceptance.

Feeling a sense of responsibility for occurrences beyond our control is a common reflex, but clinging to self-blame is a barrier to our recovery. Self-forgiveness is the act of acknowledging our humanity, our fallibility, and the finite scope of our control. It's a shift from enduring guilt as a life sentence to granting ourselves the compassion we deserve. And in this act of self-forgiveness, we do not downplay our trauma or excuse any harm caused. Rather, we choose to shed the shackles of negative emotions that bind us to pain, thereby allowing ourselves the freedom to transform and flourish.

The act of self-forgiveness invites us to look back with kindness and a discerning eye, recognizing the wisdom each past trial has bestowed upon us. It calls for us to bestow upon ourselves the empathy we'd readily extend to another in duress. Forgiveness is not a sudden retreat but a path we tread with deliberate, patient steps. As we release the binds of guilt and self-reproach linked to past times, we make room for nurturing self-love and a wholesome acceptance of ourselves. Understanding that you are not to blame for the hurt that occurred to you is a crucial step in shifting away from self-imposed guilt. Embrace this liberating truth and turn your energy towards nurturing your well-being. Remember, the relief of self-compassion and the grace of forgiveness are potent allies on your healing journey.

To summarize, the essence of forgiveness is the cornerstone of inner tranquility. Without it, we risk being ensnared in a state of emotional stasis, allowing our pain to chart a relentless course of grief. Forgiveness is the sacrament that releases us from the haunts of our history. It encourages us to step beyond the shadows of our pasts and stride into a future sculpted by our own design. Forgiveness is not merely a concession for the benefit of others; it is, most profoundly, an act of profound self-care. It is the strength drawn from acknowledging our suffering and the conscious choice to not let it engulf our spirit. In forgiving, we dissolve the bonds that entangle our hearts and minds, inviting a renewal of love, empathy, and insight. Forgiveness is not just a passage out of turmoil; it is a passage into peace and a serene existence we all yearn to embrace.

Cultivating Forgiveness: Strategies and Techniques for Practicing Forgiveness

To navigate the landscape of forgiveness, there are potent strategies and techniques at our disposal. One such pathway is the cultivation of empathy for those who have caused us pain. Stepping into their shoes, we may unearth an understanding of their actions, born not from malice, but from their own personal battles, fears, or insecurities. Acknowledging that perfection is unattainable for any of us paves the way for compassion. This approach to empathy does not excuse harm nor invalidate our feelings; it simply humanizes the offender, acknowledging their own potential struggles. This may give us a different perspective into their mindset, not to excuse their actions but to allow us to forgive.

Patience and an open heart are the cornerstones of practicing empathy. It means listening actively, without judgment, striving for comprehension rather than reaction. This creates a haven for mutual healing and growth, fostering an environment where forgiveness can flourish. Exercising empathy fosters an environment where individuals feel seen, heard, and valued. It allows us to build bridges of understanding and compassion, even in the face of differences. In a world that can often feel divided and disconnected, empathy serves as a beacon of hope. It reminds us of our shared humanity and the importance of kindness and understanding in our interactions with others.

In tandem with empathy is the practice of self-reflection and introspection. By bravely examining our own imperfections and acknowledging our missteps, we connect with that humanity. This self-awareness breeds a deeper empathy, easing the journey towards forgiving others. Recognizing that flawlessness is a myth for all allows us to nurture a compassionate mindset that is conducive to forgiveness and builds more authentic, understanding relationships.

Accepting our own fallibility forms the bedrock of forgiveness. Through this understanding, we strengthen our connections with others, laying the groundwork for relationships enriched with mutual respect and forgiveness. Indeed, self-reflection not only fosters personal forgiveness but also cements stronger relationship bonds. In essence, forgiveness is not just about letting go of past grievances; it's about building bridges of understanding and compassion. It empowers us to move forward with lighter hearts and stronger relationships based on trust, respect, and empathy. Embracing forgiveness enriches our lives by fostering harmony within ourselves and with those around us.

Additionally, the practice of mindfulness can be a powerful ally in the journey toward forgiveness. Mindfulness anchors us in the present moment, allowing us to experience our emotions with neither judgment nor attachment. This mindful awareness illuminates' feelings of resentment or anger, granting us the choice to release them with kindness. Rather than suppressing these emotions, we welcome them, fully feeling them with the understanding that they are transient and do not define our essence.

By bringing mindfulness into our daily interactions, we foster a deeper empathy and comprehension of others' suffering, nurturing a forgiving spirit. The daily integration of mindfulness—through meditation, deep breathing, or moments of reflection—cultivates a fertile ground within us where forgiveness can flourish naturally as we learn to let go of the negative.

Reframing our perspective is another potent technique in the art of forgiveness and healing. Transitioning our view from one of victimhood to empowerment, we regain authorship of our story. It's about recognizing the hurt inflicted by others while consciously deciding to release the associated negative emotions. Reframing casts forgiveness as an act of strength, not weakness. It becomes a process of learning and wisdom acquisition, reshaping our future positively. In reframing, forgiveness ceases to be about condoning another's actions; it becomes about freeing ourselves from their emotional tether.

Employing these strategies for forgiveness, we champion our emotional liberation and pave the way for growth and healing. Letting go of past grievances allows us to inhabit the present more fully, fostering healthier relationships with ourselves and others. Unresolved pain can taint our interactions, but by addressing these wounds, we present ourselves more genuinely, inviting connections rooted in trust and understanding. In essence, releasing the past opens us up to joy, peace, and love. It's an invitation to seize new opportunities for happiness and to cultivate more profound relationships based on mutual respect and care.

▌ The Emotional and Mental Benefits of Forgiving

The journey towards forgiveness, particularly after trauma, can be a conduit for significant emotional and mental transformation, leading to what is known as post-traumatic growth. While it might appear daunting to forgive amidst distress, studies have explained forgiveness as a catalyst for profound change. This act is linked to heightened mental health, diminished anxiety and depression, bolstered self-esteem, and greater satisfaction in life. Forgiveness is a declaration of our intent to not just survive but to flourish with positivity and resilience. This mental shift doesn't only enrich our inner lives but also enhances our relationships with others.

Moreover, the practice of forgiveness correlates with reinforced self-worth. By extending forgiveness, whether to others or ourselves, we nurture a sense of self-compassion and self-acceptance. This renewed sense of self can significantly boost confidence across various life facets. Ultimately, embracing forgiveness charts a course toward resilience and hopeful living. If you're wrestling with the shadows of past pains or battling feelings of anger, consider the act of forgiveness as a tranquilizer for the soul, with extensive benefits that touch every corner of your emotional and mental landscape.

The scope of forgiveness extends beyond mental and emotional realms, touching the physical as well. Research suggests that forgiveness can lower blood pressure, reduce heart rate, and strengthen immune function. Resentment and long-held grudges can amplify stress, potentially heightening blood pressure. Yet, in choosing forgiveness, we dismiss the anger and negativity that fuel stress, thus contributing to improved cardiovascular health.

The link between chronic anger and a compromised immune response is well-documented, suggesting that forgiveness can be a potent ally for our immune system, bolstering its capacity to shield us from illness. This underscores the profound synergy between our emotional states and physical health, as explored in earlier chapters. By adopting forgiveness, we not only achieve emotional catharsis but also enhance our physical well-being. Thus, forgiveness is not merely an act of humanity; it is a profound investment in our comprehensive health and vitality.

In conclusion, the journey to cultivate forgiveness is fraught with challenges, yet it is rich with emotional and mental rewards. It propels us beyond the confines of our pain, leading us towards the path of post-traumatic growth. Embracing forgiveness after trauma is akin to opening a door to a realm brimming with potential for personal transformation and enhanced emotional health. It equips us to wield our resilience against adversity, transforming our trials into springboards for positive change. By releasing our grip on old resentments and nurturing compassion for ourselves and those involved, we initiate deep-rooted personal change.

While the road to forgiveness may be paved with patience, introspection, and sustained effort, the outcomes are boundless. Choosing this pathway to recovery allows us to mend long-standing wounds, paving the way for a resurgence of joy, liberation from the chains of past burdens, and a rejuvenated sense of well-being.

Through forgiveness, we grant ourselves the gift of healing and the promise of a brighter, more fulfilling future.

▎The Awakening

There was an unmistakable clarity on the day I chose to forgive, which I previously spoke about in an earlier chapter. Carrying a burden since my youth, I, as an adult equipped with wisdom and the desire to heal, decided it was time to release the anguish that shadowed my every step. On my porch, in a moment of quiet introspection, I exhaled a breath of intention, and there, as if by divine intervention, my perpetrator appeared in the distance. A divine sign, perhaps. Peace washed over me as "I forgive you" passed my lips, and tears of profound joy marked the turning point of my life. In that instant, the chains of shame and defeat fell away, and I embraced the liberation I had long sought.

In the wake of trauma, an awakening stirs within us. It might seem unfathomable at first, but gradually, the darkness lifts, giving way to smiles, laughter, and warmth toward others. This rebirth is a powerful affirmation of the resilience inherent in the human spirit, reminding us that hope persists even through our darkest hours. We discover the strength to rise above and reclaim our joy. The journey from darkness to light is a testament to the strength and courage that resides within each of us.

Healing is a marathon, not a sprint. There will be times when old wounds resurface, tempting us back into despair. But having savored the sweetness of liberation, we can summon the strength from that memory to persevere. When your awakening beckons, embrace it as a testament to your resilience and as a beacon for your journey of self-discovery. Your past does not define you—your capacity to overcome it does.

As this new dawn breaks, you may find yourself more attuned to your emotions, recognizing triggers, and committed to self-care. This heightened awareness allows you to navigate life post-trauma with a deeper understanding of your needs and boundaries. It also brings the importance of support networks into sharp focus, reinforcing the need to engage in practices that nurture your well-being. Embracing this newfound self-awareness and prioritizing your well-being through support networks and self-care can empower you to navigate life post-trauma with resilience and understanding.

In the end, remember that within each of us lies a light waiting to outshine the darkness. This awakening is not just about moving past trauma; it's about stepping into a redefined existence, filled with courage and hope. You possess the power to heal, to thrive, and to illuminate the way for others on their path to healing. Your journey of resilience and triumph serves as a guiding light, inspiring others to face their challenges with courage and hope.

CHAPTER 6

Embracing New Beginnings

Part 1: The Foundation of New Beginnings

With the strength we've unearthed from within and the growth that's followed, we stand on the precipice of new beginnings. This next step, while tinged with both hesitation and hope, is filled with infinite potential. To embrace the future, we must first acknowledge our past, traumatic experiences included. Such acknowledgment allows us to convert these experiences into pillars of strength. The wisdom gleaned from our past lights the path to a brighter future. Your readiness to face what has been is a testament to your courage and tenacity. It's an act of determination to recognize and learn from past missteps, yet it's through this journey of reflection and acceptance that we chart a course for positive transformation.

As you move forth, envision a future radiant with the growth you've achieved by pushing your limits and searching deep within. Trust in your resilience and your ability to navigate any challenges and seize the opportunities for personal evolution that await. Approach these new beginnings with assurance, each step bringing you closer to the most authentic version of yourself. Keep your eyes set on your goals, drawing on the strength that has emerged from your trials to guide you through the healing journey.

Starting anew is an intentional act of healing, growth, and reconstruction. It requires patience, as healing from trauma is not instantaneous. Everyone's journey is distinct, with no universal blueprint for navigation. New beginnings, though intimidating, are ripe with opportunities for both personal and post-traumatic growth. They invite us to redefine ourselves, to craft a future rich with potential and hope. They call for a reframing of life perspectives, releasing the past to fully embrace the present with gratitude and openness.

During this transformative phase, setting healthy boundaries is crucial. Prioritizing self-care and recognizing your limits creates the space needed for healing. Setting boundaries is an exercise in self-honesty, discerning what is within your emotional scope and having the courage to uphold these limits. This self-preservation ensures your mental and emotional welfare, granting you the respite necessary for recovery. Remember, self-care is a vital aspect of a balanced life. By placing importance on self-care, you fortify yourself with the energy and emotional stamina needed for this healing voyage.

A new beginning after trauma is a declaration of your unyielding resolve to reclaim your narrative, find healing, and forge a hopeful future. It's a beacon of the human spirit's resilience and an encouragement to others walking a similar path. Your narrative of overcoming adversity stands as a beacon of hope, igniting courage in others facing their trials. Each advancement is a testament to personal rebirth and an inspiration to the community you touch.

The Role of Support Systems

As we tread the path of new beginnings, the role of a robust support system becomes unmistakably crucial. Such systems provide not only a comforting presence but also practical guidance and encouragement that aid us in navigating uncharted waters. Among these, a network of friends and family stands paramount, offering an empathetic ear, sage advice, and the reinforcement of our capabilities, especially when self-doubt creeps in.

Equally instrumental are mentors—those who've traversed similar paths and can illuminate our journey with their wisdom. Their shared stories and strategies act as beacons, offering bespoke solutions that help us tackle our unique challenges with greater finesse. Their guidance, support, and insight can contribute invaluable insights that help us seize opportunities and grow into the best adaptations of ourselves.

Professional support, too, plays a pivotal role. Therapists and coaches bring specialized expertise, helping to identify our strengths, set achievable goals, and develop actionable plans to surmount obstacles. Online communities based on shared interests or endeavors also serve as a rich reservoir of collective wisdom and camaraderie, providing both inspiration and pragmatic advice. Being part of such communities can be extremely beneficial as they offer a wealth of knowledge and practical tools that can enhance your understanding of your chosen path. Their guidance not only helps you avoid common pitfalls but also equips you with the necessary resources to make informed decisions about your future.

Self-support, however, should not be overlooked. Prioritizing our physical and mental health through exercise and mindfulness can significantly bolster our adaptability. Regular physical activity invigorates the body and mind, while mindfulness practices like meditation or deep breathing can enhance our inner peace, clarity, and resilience. Caring for ourselves is the cornerstone of resilience and success in navigating life's challenges. By prioritizing our physical, mental, and emotional well-being, we can build a strong foundation that equips us to face the ups and downs with grace and determination. Self-care is not a luxury but a necessity for achieving our full potential.

The confluence of these support systems—personal, professional, and self-directed—ensures that we're well-equipped for the rigors of new beginnings. Their collective strength fortifies our sense of connection and belonging as we step into the unknown. The belief others place in us can be transformative, elevating our self-confidence and highlighting our potential, even amid uncertainty. These networks of support are the foundations of our success. They stand as a testament to the power of community and self-care, urging us forward with unwavering faith in our capacity to thrive in the face of new challenges.

▌ Integrating Past Experiences

As we embark on the journey of creating new beginnings, it's essential to recognize the value of integrating our past traumas into our life's narrative. Acknowledging these experiences not only teaches us invaluable lessons but also empowers us to build a future rich in meaning. Embracing our traumas as part of our identity fosters a profound self-understanding and kindles empathy for others facing similar battles. This awareness liberates us from the chains of our pain, allowing us to repurpose our struggles into something meaningful. Our transformation of pain into purpose serves as a beacon for others, demonstrating the resilience and inner strength that we all hold within. Embrace the fact that your past traumas are not a burden but a stepping stone towards growth and healing.

In accepting our past traumas, we grant ourselves the freedom to heal and evolve. Weaving these stories into our lives lets us recast our narrative in a way that uplifts rather than constrains us. Additionally, the act of sharing our journey can profoundly touch others in search of hope or direction. By speaking candidly about integrating our traumatic experiences, we become harbingers of hope to those still in the throes of their own trials. Our capacity for empathy becomes a source of fortitude—not only for ourselves but also for those around us. Ultimately, when we engage in the practice of incorporating our past traumas into our life story with heart and sincerity, it becomes an invaluable instrument in sculpting our future selves.

Gaining control over your narrative is a pivotal step toward crafting your new beginning. It's an empowering process that lets you reclaim your story and reshape it to reflect your ambitions and dreams for the future. By owning your narrative, you become the architect of your destiny, penning your life's script, redefining your identity, and embarking on an authentic new chapter. This journey involves drawing strength from within to progress and learning from the past while freeing yourself from its hold. Transformation comes as you release negative emotions that once hindered you, clearing the way for growth and healing. Remember, controlling your narrative isn't about negating your past; it's about reshaping your experiences to fuel your empowerment.

Taking charge of your life and deciding who you want to become can unveil a realm of new possibilities. When you assume responsibility for your happiness and success, you're able to make deliberate choices that resonate with your genuine self. Redefining your identity helps you craft a clear vision of the person you're striving to be, setting meaningful goals and pursuing them with intent. It's a chance to discard outdated patterns and adopt new, supportive behaviors that foster your development. With ownership of your life comes not just fresh opportunities but also a profound sense of purpose and fulfillment. You become the creator of your future, sculpting it to match your aspirations. So, seize this moment for introspection and begin the transformative process of redefining yourself.

Take Marie's story, for example, as a narrative of integrating past experiences into a journey of new beginnings. A survivor of childhood sexual abuse, Marie spent her twenties feeling undeserving of love and joy. She sought validation and affection from anyone, often disregarding their intentions, driven by a deep-seated need to be cared for. This longing led her into an abusive relationship that nearly claimed her life. Despite numerous attempts to break free, she struggled to find the emotional strength to do so. Like many others in similar plights, she misinterpreted abuse as love, desperate for the affection she yearned for.

One transformative day, Marie found herself in the hospital, nursing a broken nose and ribs—a grim gift from another of his "loving" outbursts. It was a harrowing wake-up call, one that resonated deep within her soul, sparking the realization that this was not the life she wanted. Not long after, Marie sought out a support group, a safe haven where she could unravel her emotions and seek out positive replacements for what she had been missing. With each passing day, her strength multiplied, and eventually, she summoned the fortitude to leave the relationship behind. She described feeling almost superhuman the day she walked away.

Together, we worked on reframing her narrative, focusing on how her traumatic past could be channeled into meaningful advocacy. In just a year, Marie took her place as a volunteer in the fight against domestic violence, and within three years, she became a counselor. Her journey, powered by her own survival story, now stands as a beacon of hope for other women. Her story not only inspires but also empowers, showcasing the strength and determination that lie within each individual to overcome adversity and emerge victorious.

Marie's story epitomizes the indomitable human spirit and the regenerative power of new beginnings. Despite the darkness of her past, she discovered the light of self-healing and growth. The lessons learned—courage, self-love, and the art of forgiveness—have reshaped her identity, transforming her past into a springboard for personal evolution.

Marie didn't walk this path alone. She leaned on therapeutic communities that offered understanding and solace. These groups were instrumental in her healing, offering her validation and a chance to mend. Now, eight years later, Marie continues to cultivate relationships that lift her and enforce boundaries that protect her from past triggers. Her commitment to self-care, including mindfulness meditation and therapy, is unwavering, ensuring that her journey towards emotional health is ever-forward.

Marie's narrative stands as a beacon to all who face their own adversities. It's a testament that we can incorporate our past into a present that nourishes us, rather than holds us back. By acknowledging our history without letting it define us, we unlock doors to new realms of possibility, healing, and self-reinvention. Marie's life is a testament to resilience, the journey of self-discovery, and the grace of second chances.

▌ The Power of Resilience

Resilience is a key pillar in the journey of post-traumatic growth and recovery. It's the inner strength that enables us to overcome and adapt to the hardships wrought by trauma. Developing resilience is not just about piecing our lives back together; it's about personal evolution and finding deeper meaning in our stories. Through resilience, we gain the fortitude to conquer challenges and emerge stronger.

Self-care activities are instrumental in building our resilience as previously mentioned. Regular exercise, for example, bolsters both physical and mental health, mitigating stress and elevating our mood. Restorative sleep is essential— it rejuvenates us, equipping our minds and bodies to tackle daily challenges with renewed vigor. Meditation, too, is invaluable, quieting the mind, fostering mindfulness, and enhancing emotional regulation, all of which fortify our resilience.

Resilience serves as a fortress against life's stressors, safeguarding our mental health and enabling us to manage adversities proactively. It imbues us with adaptability and flexibility, transforming potential defeats into opportunities for growth. With resilience, we maintain a hopeful outlook and actively seek paths forward. It's also a fortification for our mental health, helping us to keep emotions in check and prevent stress from undermining our overall wellness. As we cultivate resilience, we arm ourselves with the grace to face life's uncertainties with poise and determination.

Additionally, establishing robust coping strategies is a cornerstone for sustaining resilience. Accessing therapy or counseling is a proactive step toward effectively processing trauma and acquiring stress management skills. These therapeutic avenues offer a sanctuary for unraveling emotions and thoughts, under the guidance of professionals skilled in nurturing one's journey to recovery.

Engaging with therapy or counseling can illuminate personal thought patterns and behaviors, providing valuable perspectives on the path to wellness.

Fostering a positive mindset is another critical element in fortifying resilience. It's about emphasizing our strengths, transforming challenges into growth opportunities, and expressing gratitude for each step forward, no matter how small. Recognizing even the smallest triumphs heightens our awareness of progress, fueling our motivation and reinforcing self-belief. This sense of appreciation reminds us of our capacity for achievement, despite hurdles or delays. Concentrating on accomplishments rather than outstanding tasks fosters a mindset geared towards optimism and self-assurance.

Take a moment to honor every victory. Whether it's navigating a complex situation or stepping beyond the familiar bounds of comfort, each triumph inches us closer to our overarching aspirations. Let's embrace every success as a cause for celebration, propelling us toward our greater objectives with renewed vigor.

Achieving post-traumatic growth is indeed a commendable expedition, one where nurturing self-compassion is vital. Treating yourself with kindness becomes a sanctuary, recognizing your pain and affirming your strength and right to heal. Self-compassion is that gentle nudge, reminding you that your feelings are valid in the aftermath of trauma. It's a call to patience, to allow yourself the space and time for emotional healing. Rather than succumbing to self-critique, self-compassion invites you to approach your recovery with empathy and care.

In wrapping up, the journey of building resilience in the wake of trauma is a deliberate process, one enriched by several contributing factors. Resilience is a cultivated skill, not an innate trait, honed through experience and practice. A pivotal part of this development is self-reflection—assessing the impact of trauma and understanding our emotional responses. Such awareness lays the groundwork for growth and prepares us to handle future adversities more adeptly.

By leaning into support systems, honing coping skills, nurturing positivity, and practicing self-compassion, we set the stage for a profound transformation.

This holistic approach equips us with the tools for a healing journey, guiding us towards a rediscovery of strength and a renewed sense of self.

Strategies for Goal Setting and Personal Growth

Venturing into personal growth post-trauma may seem overwhelming, yet with the proper mindset and actionable strategies, it's entirely feasible to set and accomplish significant goals. Below are practical steps designed to guide you through your journey of post-traumatic growth:

1. **Reflect on Your Experiences:** Delve into your past trauma and its impact on you. Such contemplation lays the groundwork for setting goals that resonate with your core values and future ambitions.

2. **Specific and Realistic Goals:** Craft precise goals that mirror your personal growth and aspirations. They should be achievable within a reasonable period to foster a sense of progress.

3. **Smaller Milestones:** Break your larger goals into more manageable sub-goals. This segmentation allows for effective tracking and helps sustain your drive.

4. **SMART Framework:** Apply the SMART (Specific, Measurable, Attainable, Relevant, Time-bound) criteria to each goal, ensuring clarity and measurability.

5. **Action Plan:** Map out specific actions needed to reach your goals. Anticipate potential hurdles and devise solutions to navigate them.

6. **Support Network:** Cultivate a circle of individuals who support and understand personal growth endeavors. Sharing goals with them can offer you additional accountability and inspiration.

7. **Celebrate Progress:** Recognize and honor every achievement, no matter how minor, as they are significant markers on your path to growth.

8. **Acknowledge Setbacks:** Accept setbacks as part of the growth process, not indicators of failure, but as chances to learn and strengthen resilience.

9. **Adaptive Goals:** Regularly re-evaluate your goals to ensure they remain aligned with your evolving circumstances and insights gained during your healing.

Establishing defined, actionable goals is pivotal to personal growth and self-improvement. With a clear vision, you can navigate purposefully towards your objectives. By delineating your goals, you forge a roadmap that steers your self-improvement journey, breaking down grand aspirations into attainable tasks.

Each progressive step takes you nearer to your ultimate goals, transforming personal growth into tangible strides that reinforce resilience and empowerment. Witnessing your own advancement bolsters confidence and fortifies your belief in the attainable. Remember, the essence of self-improvement lies not in perfection but in persistent advancement. Celebrate the distance you've traversed and maintain faith in the journey that unfolds. Persist with resolve, knowing each effort is instrumental in sculpting the finest version of yourself.

Part 3: Facing Reality and Moving Forward

▎ Healing vs. Masking

True healing from trauma is a cornerstone of personal growth and well-being. However, it's not uncommon to sidestep this vital process, masking the trauma instead of confronting it. We need to understand the dangers of bypassing healing and recognize whether we are genuinely recovering or simply concealing our wounds. Masking trauma, whether deliberate or not, can extend our suffering and impede the journey to post-traumatic growth. Burying the pain might seem the easier route, but it can delay the healing process and hinder the achievement of our goals.

When we mask our trauma, we're presenting a façade that all is well, yet beneath the surface, unresolved issues persist. These can manifest as anxiety, depression, low self-esteem, anger, or even physical illness. Ignoring these signs and pretending they're nonexistent blocks the path to authentic healing and growth.

There are several risks associated with masking versus healing trauma:

1. **Delayed Emotional Recovery:** Avoiding the confrontation of trauma can result in a postponement of emotional recovery. Suppressed emotions and memories might offer a temporary reprieve, giving a false impression of resolution. However, these feelings can reemerge, leading to mood swings, persistent sadness, or avoidance behaviors.

2. **Unresolved Core Issues:** Masking trauma prevents us from addressing the fundamental issues reshaped by our traumatic experiences. This avoidance can stunt personal growth and self-understanding. Indicators of unresolved core issues may include self-destructive behaviors, avoidance of triggering situations, or continuous negative self-talk.

3. **Physical Manifestations:** Unaddressed trauma can lead to physical symptoms, as our mental state significantly influences our physical health. Chronic stress from unresolved trauma can weaken the immune system and exacerbate health problems. Symptoms might include persistent headaches, digestive issues, sleep disturbances, or unexplained fatigue.

Recognizing the signs of masked trauma is essential. True healing requires us to face and process our trauma. If you notice signs of delayed recovery, unresolved issues, or physical symptoms linked to trauma, consider seeking professional help or engaging in healing practices. Trained professionals can assist in processing emotions, identifying triggers, and establishing coping strategies. They provide a supportive environment for working through the core issues that might be restraining your progress.

▌ Facing Reality: The Hard Truth

Standing before the mirror, we must pose ourselves the tough questions. Have we truly engaged with the healing process, or have we merely pretended, wandering through it with eyes closed? Have we distanced ourselves from our trauma, or have we confronted it with courage? Until we can answer these questions with an unwavering "YES," we cannot fully embrace new beginnings and risk tumbling back into that darkness we've fought so hard to escape.

Reflecting on your healing journey is a vital exercise. It's essential to recognize that healing is not a uniform process; it is deeply personal and varies from one individual to another. Some may dive into the healing process, while others may struggle, feeling as if they're groping in the dark. Yet, it's the ebb and flow, the peaks and valleys, that carve the path to wholeness. Trust in your ability to disentangle from the web of trauma, for even amidst uncertainty, you are building strength and resilience.

For some, stepping back from trauma serves as a shield, a buffer against the sting of raw memories. For others, healing requires a direct confrontation with the pain, perhaps through therapy or support, and working diligently through the discomfort. The quest to find meaning and purpose is paramount in fostering personal growth and forging new beginnings. We must probe the depths of our experiences, grasp their influence on us, and harness this understanding to chart a positive course ahead.

Facing the dark nights—the rebound moments—is not merely a challenge; it's a portal to self-discovery and change, demanding honesty and a readiness to grow. It's a formidable task, but it's through these trials that we evolve. Embrace these challenges; they are the crucibles within which personal growth is refined. It is a journey of self-exploration and introspection that can lead to profound personal growth and self-awareness.

In the throes of hardship, recognition of our experiences and their influence is key. Self-reflection unravels insights into our character, laying bare our strengths and vulnerabilities. It's this understanding that guides our conscious choices as we stride forward. Instead of perceiving difficulties as setbacks, we can reinterpret them as fertile ground for personal enrichment and self-mastery. They compel us to recalibrate our life's compass, to ponder again on our aspirations, and to redefine what triumph truly means to us. Every hurdle surmounted and lesson absorbed fortifies us. Transformation germinates from the intent to change and the actions that follow. It may mean choosing our companions wisely or cultivating new skills and habits that resonate with our future selves. Remember, personal transformation is an ongoing odyssey, not a finishing point. It asks for patience, tenacity, and a gentle hand towards oneself. By welcoming the dark nights as catalysts for growth, we lay down stepping stones to a future radiant with possibility. Let us delve into our stories with an embracing spirit and unleash their metamorphic power.

▍Moving Forward: A World Beyond the Pain

Envision a future where the shadows of past traumas no longer dictate your boundaries, where

the odyssey of healing has begun, and personal growth is blooming. Picture a life where the anguish has been left behind and you stand in the glow of hope, resilience, and endless potential. In this future, your triumphs over the trials of yesterday have forged you into a being of strength and vibrancy. Each step you take is a dance, casting off the heavy chains of the past and spinning into the embrace of newfound liberty. This isn't merely a daydream; it's a future within grasp, awaiting your steadfast commitment to nurturing your well-being, uncovering your innermost self, and seizing your power.

Hold this vision close and let it be the beacon that lights your way toward a future brimming with joy and steadfast resolve. Let it serve as a constant reminder that you are capable of rising above, transforming fragility into fortitude. Trust in the unwavering power of your spirit and the limitless opportunities that beckon. Regard each challenge as a stepping stone for growth, each obstacle as a testament to your enduring strength. With tenacity and courage, navigate your life towards a horizon of fulfillment. Happiness is not just a transient state; it's a sanctuary built upon the small, yet profound joys of life—laughter, love, and heartfelt gratitude.

In moments of doubt or sorrow, grip tightly to this inspiring vision. Let it propel you, a reminder of the formidable strength that resides within. You are equipped with all the tools necessary to surmount any barrier that may arise. During times of uncertainty, it is easy to lose sight of our capabilities and succumb to self-doubt. However, by embracing this empowering perspective, we can tap into our inner resilience and face any challenges that seek to hinder us.

This future, radiant with promise, is not a far-off dream, but an achievable reality, accessible through steadfast effort and commitment. Envision a life where happiness blossoms, where each forward stride is met with satisfaction, not sadness. Stand tall amidst adversity, buoyed by an indomitable belief in your capabilities. This future is within reach; it begins with an unwavering pledge to foster your holistic growth.

As we close this chapter on embracing new beginnings and armed with actionable strategies, excuses fall away. We're ready to nurture supportive bonds and cultivate the resilience that will carry us forward. With this renewed vigor, we set goals that will further our personal evolution, propelling us into the next chapter of our healing journey. As you turn the page, bring along the fortitude, wisdom, and valor you've garnered. Your journey through post-traumatic growth is a saga of resilience; continue to thrive.

"The beginning is the most important part of the work."

~ Plato

CHAPTER 7

Relationships and Connection

Stronger Together: The Power of Healing Relationships

All right, now that we're on this wild ride towards new beginnings after trauma, it's time to talk about the real game-changers: our relationships and connections with others. I'm not just talking out of my backside here - when the going gets tough, having solid people in your corner can make all the difference.

Let me lay it out for you - in the face of serious strife, a strong support system is like a life raft. Those real-deal friends, family, or even professionals who truly hear you and get what you're going through? That's pure gold, my friend. Being able to open up, vent, and let those emotions flow without judgment is healing in itself. But it goes deeper than that - working through the hard stuff with people who've been there, showcasing that beautiful human empathy? That's where the magic happens.

Having that circle who's got your back makes you feel safe and like you belong. It's powerful to know there are folks who care enough to stand by you through the grittiest times. That security allows you to really dig in and do the work of moving forward. And sometimes, it's those loved ones who inspire you most. Hearing how they climbed out of their own hell can reignite that inner spark of hope and resilience within yourself.

I'm getting a little sappy here, but the rawness of human connection is what it's all about for me. Being able to authentically share your story, fears, dreams - the whole enchilada - with someone you trust implicitly? That vulnerability breeds healing. An open heart and mind between two people are a sacred space for growth. Judging from my own experiences, those real, ride-or-die relationships have been vital on this journey towards light after darkness.

So, to anyone out there feeling alone in their struggle - I see you, and I've been there. But I'm telling you, placing your trust in the right handful of remarkable humans can literally change everything. The path isn't easy but walking it hand-in-hand with your personal life rafts makes it infinitely more bearable. Nurture those bonds, let your guard down with those who have earned it, and watch how that honest connection transforms you.

For the longest time, I was stuck stumbling down that isolated road, cutting myself off from any meaningful connections. I thought I could white-knuckle my way through the pain alone, that opening up would just make me weaker. Boy, was I dead wrong about that? See, I had this core belief that trusting people was a liability. My experiences had burned that mentality deep into me - let folks in, and they'll only disappoint, abandon, or hurt you in the end. So, I closed myself off, living in that lonely bubble thinking it was protecting me. But really? I was just compounding the trauma, letting it fester unchecked without any support system to lean on.

While I plowed through each day wearing that tough exterior, inside, I was an absolute mess—a hot cauldron of unprocessed emotions and turmoil slowly corroding me from the inside out. Without anyone to share that burden with, to lend an understanding ear, or a reassuring hug, the weight just became more and more unbearable over time.

I wish I could go back and shake some sense into my stubborn self because it took way too long for me to learn this vital truth: We need bonding and nurturing relationships to heal our deepest wounds. Our souls crave that human intimacy and connection like a dying plant craves water. Depriving ourselves of that basic need only perpetuates the cycle of hurt. Once I finally swallowed my pride and started letting a few good people in, everything shifted. Having a support system to catch me when I stumbled, to celebrate the tiny wins with me, to simply remind me that I wasn't alone in this fight? It was a total game-changer. Real healing could finally take root within those bonds of trust and compassion.

Repair, Reconnect, Rebuild: Healing Broken Bonds

Trauma, man...it's like a wrecking ball straight through your life, leveling any sense of security or trust you had in relationships. I know that devastation all too well from personal experience. When you've been through something that shatters your core, everything gets thrown out of whack - especially the bonds with those closest to you. Suddenly you're struggling with letting people in, being vulnerable, even just having basic faith that others genuinely care. An isolating loneliness creeps in as you instinctively start walling yourself off.

It's a vicious cycle too, because that very isolation ends up breeding more trauma. You get caught in these anxiety loops, endlessly replaying the pain, stuck in the same fractured patterns with loved ones because you're terrified of confronting the rawness. Pretty soon, the slightest things - a familiar smell, a certain tone of voice - become triggering landmines that blow up in your face.

I can't even count how many times I completely overreacted or shut down on people over some seemingly innocent remark that somehow linked back to my trauma vault. The confusion in their eyes will forever haunt me. They were desperately trying to understand, to help...but I was so tangled in my own mind that I could barely process their attempt to understand. I shied away from even explaining it out of fear of their disapproval which was all in my head. They longed to understand what I was going through, but I didn't have the strength to comply.

That's the cruelest part about trauma's shockwaves through relationships - the people who love you most can end up becoming unintentional casualties. Trust erodes, and communication breaks down into infinite misunderstandings when you're both just fighting different sides of the same war. Before you know it, you're trapped in this emotional rubble wondering how you'll ever rebuild something so broken.

That first step of repair work is crucial, but it's just laying the foundation. The real heavy lifting comes when you take that initial progress and start reconnecting with the very people your trauma forced you to shut out. Reaching out and rebuilding connections with others can be the most challenging yet rewarding part of the healing process. It allows us to not only mend broken relationships but also to create new ones based on a stronger foundation of understanding.

I'm not going to lie - reaching back out to folks you've isolated, asking for another chance after hurting them...it's scary as hell. Digging up all that regret and pain, making yourself vulnerable again when self-protection was your coping mechanism for so long? It requires an incredible amount of courage to push through that fear. But here's the truth: that courage is what unlocks the door to profound healing and growth. Reconnecting, truly reestablishing those severed bonds, is a radical act of self-love. It's you saying "I want to be whole again. I'm ready to face the wreckage I created during my darkest moments."

For me, taking that courageous first step involved having a heart-to-heart conversation about my trauma with my family members. It seemed to put a strain on our relationship after years of hiding my feelings, silently lashing out, and keeping my true feelings concealed as I descended into my trauma pit. With trepidation, I finally opened up about the darkness I had been consumed by, taking responsibility for how I may have had resentment for the forced bond that involved me hiding what happened to me. Once the floodgates opened and my truth oozed out like a dam breaking, I began to see where I was wrong in my actions by not trusting them with my truth.

Their response to me? "Lisa, we've known all along that something happened; we just didn't know what it was. We have your back, and we will never stop fighting for you." I realized then how my disconnection had been slowly changing our dynamics. That conversation and their unconditional reply were a rebirth for our relationship but, most importantly, my healing. I was free from the shame and anguish that weighed me down for so many years. I was seen and heard, something that had never happened to me after my trauma.

From there, it became a conscious practice of communicating through the hard stuff with honesty and humility. Setting new boundaries and having the conversations we had avoided for far too long - it was grueling at times. But with each layer of emotional intimacy, we peeled back, our foundation was being rebuilt stronger than before. Our connection today has transcended what we even had pre-trauma - it's utterly unbreakable. I bask in the notion and am saddened by it at the same time. I could have enveloped myself in this feeling a long time ago, yet I chose to travel that rocky terrain alone. Guess what? I know now that communication and honesty are a must in your healing journey. Letting people in is crucial to your progress so don't be foolish like I was all those years ago. Embrace the inevitable, trust in the people you love and who love you.

❚ Bonding with positive people

A pivotal factor contributing to your remarkable journey towards post-traumatic growth is the mindful act of intentionally surrounding ourselves with an abundant circle of positive, empathetic, and genuinely supportive people. These extraordinary beings serve as a source of strength and play an instrumental role in assisting us in mending our emotional fences and guiding us toward healing and growth. Their unwavering support serves as a beacon of light during challenging times, uplifting our spirits and reminding us of the incredible resilience we possess within ourselves. These people not only provide us with the emotional support we need but also help us cultivate a more optimistic mindset.

When we intentionally choose to be around people who exude positivity, their energy will profoundly impact our well-being. They offer understanding, compassion, and encouragement during challenging times, which helps us navigate through our traumas and heal. Furthermore, being surrounded by truly supportive individuals means having people who genuinely believe in our potential for growth. They see beyond our past experiences and empower us to embrace new opportunities.

Additionally, these positive influences will also inspire us to adopt healthier habits and coping mechanisms. Through their example, they show us how resilience is possible even in the face of adversity. By witnessing their journeys of growth, we become motivated to embark on our own transformative path. It reinforces the belief that we are not alone in our struggles and that there is immense strength in connecting with others who share similar experiences or offer unconditional support. So, let's proactively seek out those who uplift us emotionally and mentally. Their presence in our lives will infuse us with renewed energy and a sense of purpose.

Positive people have the ability to challenge us to think beyond our comfort zones, pushing us to strive for greatness. Through their encouragement and support, we gain the confidence to pursue our dreams. Moreover, these emotionally and mentally uplifting people remind us of our own strength and resilience. They remind us that setbacks are temporary hurdles that can be overcome through perseverance and determination. These inspiring individuals serve as a constant source of motivation, reminding us of the power we hold within ourselves. They demonstrate that no matter how challenging life may seem, we have the ability to rise above adversity and achieve greatness.

Those with an optimistic outlook on their lives show us that setbacks are not permanent roadblocks but stepping stones toward personal growth and success. By sharing their experiences and triumphs, these uplifting individuals empower us to believe in our own abilities. Their unwavering determination serves as a shining example, urging us to never give up on our dreams and teach us valuable life lessons. Through their stories, we learn about resilience, self-belief, and the importance of having a positive mindset. They inspire us to cultivate inner strength and develop the mental fortitude necessary to overcome obstacles. They instill a sense of hope within us and reinforce the idea that anything is possible with hard work and dedication. So, let's surround ourselves with these amazing souls who uplift our spirits and remind us of our own potential. Let's draw inspiration from their journeys as we navigate through life's challenges with renewed optimism and determination.

▍Find your Community: Join a Club or Volunteer

You know, one of the most transformative steps on my journey was getting off my isolated island and joining a community that truly got me. After all that time surviving in survivalist mode, it was a total revelation to be surrounded by people who just innately understood the depth of my struggles without me having to overexplain myself.

I remember walking into that first group meeting, feeling so anxious and vulnerable, bracing for judgment. But from the second I started sharing my story, I was instantly wrapped by this magic bubble of empathy, compassion, and "me too" head nods all around the circle. The weight of not having to go it entirely alone anymore was indescribable.

Through that crew, I learned I wasn't a freak or a lost cause like that malicious voice in my head had been convincing me. We were all warriors who had been battered by life in some way but were still standing and fighting like hell to come out on the other side stronger. The bonds we forged overflowed with unspoken understanding, unconditional support, and so many transformative "a-ha" moments of self-discovery.

That's the true heart-opening power of community and family—finding your tribe of people who will commit to walking beside you through the grey muck without judgment or platitudes. It's a soft place to fall and have your darkest moments received with "I feel you, and you've got this" type of energy. With cheerleaders like that in your corner, you start believing in yourself again.

Those group gatherings became my weekly soul fuel. We'd share wins and setbacks with total rawness, lift each other up, and inspire one another to stay the course. The consistent group accountability gave me that extra nudge I needed to keep putting one foot in front of the other. And knowing there were people I could turn to 24/7 with a simple text when survival mode tried to kick back in? Game. Changer.

▌ The Invitation to Wise Minds and Caring Witnesses

Listen, I feel you on how frightening it can be to open up about your trauma journey with others. That fear of being judged, misunderstood, or inadvertently triggered is mad real. We've all had those well-meaning loved ones say the wrong thing at the wrong time, despite their best intentions.

But through my own healing process, I've learned that having the right soul witnesses by your side can be utterly transformative. I'm talking about those precious humans who hold space for your vulnerability without an ounce of judgment or unsolicited advice-slinging.

The type of ride-or-die crew who may not fully understand the depths of your lived experience, but who are willing to lean in, listen intently, and embrace your truth with open hearts. Companions who can sit with you in the tangled brushes of emotion and bear witness to your bravery in working through it all. I found this recently in a few good friends of mine. While I've always had my sisters and built-in best friends, Rosalyn (Roz), Robin (Monie), and Roshall (Shall), my new support system emerged through my best friends Shana and Amonie.

My closest friends took the humble student role, too, seeking first to understand rather than trying to fix me. They checked their egos and criticisms about my sometimes abusive personality and just showed up, no matter how heavy it got, allowing me to wise-mind through my hairiest triggers and trust that their love was unconditional.

For me, surrounding myself with these wise and caring presences made such a profound difference. It gave me the courage to feel confident in who I was as a friend, and I finally felt confident that someone other than my sisters had my back. This was and is still to this day a feeling I never thought I would ever experience. Through healing and self-discovery, I can finally allow my true self to shine, and they all (my sisters and my friends) understand the road I traveled to get here and play an instrumental role in validating me.

Another source of catharsis for me is having a therapist who created that sacred container where I could blurt out the rawest stuff without filter and explore the darkest shadows that trauma casts—that level of safety cracked me wide open to do the real inside work required.

With the right support system bearing witness and holding that space, I found the courage to keep addressing things that had been too horrendous to speak out loud before. And in giving voice to those unspeakable experiences, I was able to metabolize and work through their residue energetically.

So, while the journey is undoubtedly hard as hell, I can't encourage you enough to be selective about who you let into your inner sanctum during this transformational time. Invest in the relationships that feel like an energetic match for where you're at. Let your soul pick the ideal traveling companions to share the load.

▌ Your Tribe Awaits, Blazing with Belonging

Listen up, my friends - I'm going to keep preaching this gospel until it sinks in. Cultivating your supportive, soul-nourishing tribe is not just encouraged, it's utterly vital for your healing journey. Deprive yourself of that connective lifeline any longer and you're deliberately stunting your growth.

I spent years toughing it out in isolated shame and stubborn pride, convinced I could somehow push through the trauma tendrils alone. All I achieved was getting tangled up in those knotted vines of stuckness, stagnation, and a soul-sucking disconnection from anything resembling hope or light. But then the truth finally cracked my calloused heart wide open - we are wired to thrive through the bonds of spiritual familyhood, united in our shared humanity. Rejecting or withholding ourselves from that essential belonging is akin to a flower denying its need for sunlight and nutrients. An act of self-deprivation that can only breed emptiness.

So, I'm here to urgently remind you, with the full force of my being, that your people are already gathering in readiness to receive you. Crafting that sacred circle of trust, empathy, and unconditional embrace where you can finally unhook from the trauma tapes of unworthiness or being "too much" is essential. Your soul-fam who will bear witness to your shadows AND your radiantly unfolding wholeness without flinching. People who can discern when to lovingly call forth your highest self, while allowing that authentic vulnerability to come flowing out in all its beautiful, messy truth.

From within that enveloping tribe where you know you are seen, held, and cherished for your infinitely resilient essence? That's where the real alchemical healing begins to smolder. Transforming your hardships into the wildfire of passionate purpose that can illuminate the world. I vow to you - your belonging, your soul's homecoming has already been prepared with ceremonial care. The summons has rung out across all planes. Choose to hear that rallying call and let it guide you home to the warmth of your clan's drumming heartbeat. Because it's only from that wombspace of unconditional love that your phoenix rising can truly take flight.

Question: Did you cultivate healthy relationships after experiencing your trauma? Did you make stronger connections to your community?

"Your life does not get better by chance.
It gets better by change."

~ Jim Rohn

CHAPTER 8

The Healing Power of Therapy and Support Navigating the Road with Others

Exploring Therapeutic Pathways: Finding the Right Therapy for You

All right, now, at this point, I consider you as my family. Let's get raw about this therapy game for a second. In the aftermath of trauma's gut punches, having a solid guide to navigate those murky emotional waters is pretty damn invaluable. I'm talking about someone who can hold that sacred space for you to do the real fundamentals work of unpacking your psyche's baggage.

But here's the real deal - not every therapy path is going to vibe with your unique soul blueprint. How you choose to explore those inner landscapes and heal what's been fractured is an intensely personal journey. You've got to take the time to mindfully feel out what methods and modalities best align with your goals and preferences.

For some, that might mean leaning into talking, deep-diving psychotherapy to really excavate and analyze those childhood wounds. Others might resonate more with somatic or energy-focused practices that allow stuck emotions to be released through the physical vessel. And for folks like me, a fusion of multiple approaches was key to holistic progress.

I remember my first stint in therapy feeling sort of meh. The conventional talk therapy methods weren't quite cracking the code to unlock my body's held traumas. That's when I started selectively adding in breathwork, EMDR processing, and even some shamanic sound healing - basically anything to help me get out of my defensive head and into feeling those wonderful sensations fully.

Through intuiting and customizing my own therapeutic cocktail, complete with occasional "woo" ingredients, I finally started experiencing breakthroughs. Viscerally discharging emotional residue that had been stuck in my nervous system for decades. Metabolizing layers of childhood conditioning that had me unconsciously self-sabotaging all areas of life.

It wasn't always a graceful process, mind you. There were intense sessions that had me ugly crying all the repressed anguish out. Others that triggered me into pride-cloaked rages as I fought my own healing. But with trustworthy guides to support and bear witness, I could stay committed.

Ultimately, creatively exploring the diverse therapeutic buffet available was an invaluable part of reclaiming my sovereignty. By turning inward and truly listening to what my being craved, I discovered the remedies and curated the transformational inner work that allowed me to reauthor my entire narrative. Therapy was a breath of fresh air all while scaring the bejesus out of me. I didn't know if the walls of my misfortune would come tumbling down and crush me or if the winds of redemption would blow my worries away giving way to a clean slate. It turns out to be my saving grace and I will forever be grateful.

Now that we've gotten radically honest about the profoundly personal nature of this healing journey, let's explore some of the diverse therapeutic offerings available for us to selectively sample.

We've got our classic talk therapy routes like CBT and psychodynamic approaches. For those craving a cerebral deep dive into reimprinting childhood programming and unpacking cognitive patterns, these can provide an amazing foundation. Personally, I loved having that dedicated space to just blurt out my spiraling thoughts without a filter until the threads began to unravel themselves.

But being the spiritually eccentric creature that I am, I also needed to explore the vast scope of complementary modalities that engage the body on a somatic, quasi-mystical level. Breathwork, sound healing, trance-induced parts work... basically any portal that allowed me to drop out of my defensive head and directly experience the energy of trapped emotions as felt sense.

EMDR was really pivotal for me in metabolizing specific traumatic memories too. Being able to objectively witness and reprocess those gut-punching scenes from a more liberated headspace? Life-altering. It created room for the tender parts of my psyche to finally reveal what they had encoded as coping mechanisms all those years.

At the end of the day, I'm a firm believer that no single therapeutic approach has a monopoly on healing. We're multidimensional beings, making customized cocktails using whatever medicine speaks to our soul's truth is where it's at. Maybe for you, that looks like fusing Jungian analysis with somatic movement practices. Or indigenous plant rituals used in horticultural therapy combined with polyvagal meditations. I don't have the recipe - only you can understand what your being craves to unearth and combine the ancient psychic imprints.

So, stay open and explore without judgment. It's through self-honoring that curious path of therapeutic enrichment that we unhook the limiting beliefs and stories to reclaim our true essence. And who knows—those modalities that first felt inaccessible or too "out there" may ultimately reveal themselves as our most profound gateways to healing.

The Strength of Support Groups: Harnessing Collective Healing

All right, so we've talked about the intimate journey of carving your own personalized therapeutic path. But there's another next-level game-changer I need to shout from the rooftops - the healing power of being held in the embrace of your "soul squad" (support groups) through all those inner digs. I'm talking about joining forces with a supportive crew who just get it on a cellular level because they've been wading through similar depths themselves. A tribe of kindred journeyers who are willing to bear witness without judgment, celebrate each hard-earned victory with you, and quite literally help transform stagnant energies into activated growth simply by showing up in a circle together.

There's a profound, almost mystical transformation that occurs when you gather with people who've stared into the same shadowy abyss you have. This unspoken resonance immediately bypasses all need for overwrought explanation about where you're at or why. In those bonded moments of feeling so deeply understood, a quintessential piece of healing interlocks into place.

For me, my women's trauma group during those first courageous years of exploration was utterly invaluable. Having that dedicated space where I could peel back layers upon layers of raw vulnerability without fear - it allowed an emotional honesty to pour out that solo therapy sometimes couldn't quite access. The tears, the rage releases, the sacrilegious laughing jags over our shared unstable humanity...we spiraled all the way down together before midwifing each other's rebirth.

So, while your solitary inner work is sacred, don't deprive yourself of the exponential growth that occurs when you unite your journey with aligned others in group therapy. The collective energies you generate through that depth of seenness and belonging are nothing short of wildly transformative, co-catalyzing deeper awakenings that might never flower through sheer personal effort alone. The bonds and relationships that are forged through group therapy is a life-altering experience that becomes a welcomed tool in your tool chest of survival.

Now I'd be remiss if I didn't lift up one of the most transcendent recent evolutions in the support group realm - the rise of online/virtual gatherings. These digital sanctuaries are opening up gateways to human connection that shatter boundaries of geography and circumstance. In this digital era, online groups provide a sense of community and belonging that was once confined to in-person interactions. You can share your stories, seek advice, and offer empathy within the confines of your personal space, making support more accessible than ever before. The convenience of online platforms allows you to engage at your own pace and comfort level, fostering inclusivity and understanding among diverse individuals.

For so many of us navigating life's most spiritually incendiary terrains, the ability to hop into a video portal and instantly land amidst our fellow travelers is transcending. It's a game-changer that would have seemed like sci-fi fantasy just a couple of decades ago. But now this beautiful, bleeding-edge option exists for anyone who might be location-bound, chronically ill, or simply craving that supplemental soul-sustenance between IRL meetups.

Obviously, there are some inherent limitations to this format. Physical proximity and energetic attunement undergo a distinct translation when everything is filtered through a screen. Those subtle layers of body language, eye contact, and energetic exchange - can feel a bit dampened through the digital mirror. But you'd be amazed at the depth of intimacy still accessible when you gather a crew of genuine, courageously open-hearted humans in any kind of circle container, even a virtual one.

It all flows back to that central tenet - we humans are divinely hardwired to thrive through the nutrient-rich bonds of conscious community, in whatever novel form that sacred vessel takes. So, while digital forums come with their own unique considerations around building true cohesion, I'm immensely grateful this option continues expanding to meet people exactly where they're at.

Because at the end of the day, the method or medium matters less than the intention. It's about bringing an energetic continuity to the work. A seamless bridge between the solos inner excavations and reigniting amongst one's people when the spirit longs for that restoring group significance. Protecting that sacred feedback loop ultimately allows the deepest revelations to transcend.

Family and Friends: Leveraging Personal Relationships in Recovery

We've dived deep into exploring all the outer wellsprings of therapeutic nourishment - from somatic soul midwives to heart-blazing virtual circles. But there's an entirely other dimension of support that can't be overlooked on this journey back to wholeness. I'm talking about the intimate, purgative grace that can be channeled through tapping into your nearest and dearest personal bonds.

See, while therapists and meaningful groups are invaluable, excavating the ancient suffering we've suppressed, and illuminating new pathways forward... that elevated work doesn't happen in a vacuum. Having your emotional ecosystem cultivated and reinforced by loved ones who have a driving stake in your wellbeing? That's where the deepest integration and embodiment get planted.

For an extended period in my personal history, filled with challenges, I decided to shield my friends and family from witnessing the depth of my inner struggles. In an attempt to appear strong and resilient, I concealed my pain behind a facade of false positivity, believing it was safer to portray myself as a survivor. However, this misguided approach only served to build barriers of isolation and detachment between myself and the individuals who had always cherished me unconditionally since the beginning of time.

It was only when I summoned the courage to embark on the profound journey of vulnerability, inviting my innermost circle back into my life, shedding off layers of protective armor, and vulnerably sharing the deeply buried narratives of my past, that a transformative process began to unfold at a cellular level within me. Dormant connections that had withered away were rejuvenated and reinstated to their inherent vibrancy. In a remarkable shift, I found myself immersed in a sea of unwavering love and acceptance echoing back at me from all directions.

In the moments of vulnerability, those compassionate souls didn t feel the pressure to provide all the answers or wise advice. Their mere presence, as unwavering and non-judgmental witnesses, acted as a soothing comfort for the soul. It was a poignant reminder that even in the depths of my struggles, I was not defined by my darkest moments but rather by the brightness that resided within me. Their ability to gaze unflinchingly into my darkness and still perceive the eternal light of perfection radiating through is a testament to their empathy and understanding.

Therefore, if you have individuals in your personal circle who have proven themselves to be indispensable allies on this journey of integration, do not hesitate to welcome them with open arms as you navigate through the intricate and transformative process of your ongoing evolution. These deep-rooted connections serve as the vital link that guides you back to a state of completeness and balance, reinforcing the significance of shared experiences in nurturing your growth and well-being.

▌ My Therapeutic Journey

Take into account my story. I didn't get the opportunity to engage in individual or group therapy until I was in my late thirties. I didn't get to utilize my family and friends either because you were taught to keep your business to yourself when I was growing up. I was well into my profession as a therapist yet had no firsthand experience of what benefits therapy possessed. I remember experiencing a setback when I was thirty-six years old. I started reliving those old feelings of self-doubt and insecurity like I did when I was a child. My relationship started to suffer and I began to retreat back into the confounding chrysalis that once held me captive. I sought out a therapist who was completely opposite of me, which means she was white and in her sixties. This made me wildly uncomfortable.

At first, I thought it was a waste of my fractured time. She would spew out the same questions I did with my patients, which unconsciously was a well-rehearsed script to me. After about six weeks of sessions filled with recalling the incidents and exploring my feelings, she asked me to do an exercise I was all too familiar with. We were about to engage in what is called " the empty chair" technique. In this exercise, the person in therapy sits across from an empty chair, which represents the perpetrator, aggressor, or maybe even part of themselves they are at odds with. The therapist encourages conversation between the person in therapy and the person or thing the chair represents. It's a back-and-forth conversation with the person in therapy playing both parts. The goal is to address unresolved feelings or past conflicts within you by bringing the emotions into the present and working through them in that moment.

Unbeknownst to me this would be the day I would have the breakthrough of a lifetime. I sat across from the chair, envisioning my perpetrator and just haphazardly started to have a conversation. I asked questions like "Why would you do this?" or "What did I do to deserve this?" or many other stifled queries I've stored inside of myself and something started to manifest externally. Tears began to cascade down my face as I yelled convincingly to the person in the other chair. It became genuine. I answered back with just as much vigor and began to cry in my role as the perpetrator. I felt both entities' pain and torment. This barrage went on for what seemed like hours. Once I was done, I sat there swaying back and forth, hugging myself. Not my thirty-six-year-old self but my eleven-year-old self. I could see her as plain as day in my mind, she was in that room absorbing all of the words she'd longed to hear at her most vulnerable point.

At the end of the session, I felt a weight lifted from me. The heavy saddle I didn't know I was carrying around with me. I felt resurrected and ready to yell from the mountain tops, "I'm free." See, I thought I was free when I forgave my perpetrator, but that session freed me from myself. From all of my self-sabotage, my self-loathing, my self-harm. I was emboldened to minister if you will, the power of emotional release. Emotional release is also referred to as a catharsis or emotional cleansing. It refers to gaining mastery over negative feelings and moods. Sometimes, this happens organically, like when you feel stress building then break down and cry. It feels terrible, but then the release leaves you with a sense of peace. I couldn't wait to use this technique on more of my clients now that I had firsthand experience. From then on, I became in tune with who I was and what I wanted out of life. I was emotionally empowered, and my elevation and transformation soared to new heights. I became ME.

As I wrote this, that amazing sensation came over me again. This is a testament that therapy can be a healthy option on your road to post-traumatic healing. Now that we have identified a few types of therapy, including groups, we can be empowered to move forward. We can invest in our recovery by embracing our friends and family as support to help us along the way. I know it seems scary, or you may not 100% trust in its benefits, but it wouldn't hurt to try. You can never experience the authentic effects of something if you are not open to trying new things. Take a leap of faith and start exploring therapists and groups today. What's the worst that could happen?

"The first step towards getting somewhere is to decide you're not going to stay where you are."

~J.P. Morgan

CHAPTER 9

A Long-Term View: Living and Growing Beyond Trauma

Stories of Sustained Growth: Real-Life Examples of Long-Term Recovery

When you're being engulfed by trauma's lingering powers, it can feel like the darkest of unbearable nights will never end. Like the way forward is hopelessly obscured and all that awaits is a continuance of suffering. But I'm here to emanate a spark of gentle reassurance - the dawn's first light is always inevitable if you simply stay present and keep putting one foot in front of the other. Healing and wholeness await you, no matter how endless the void may feel at this moment.

To illuminate that truth, I'm going to share some real-life stories of determined individuals who have walked through their own harrowing times into the triumphal sunrise of long-term post-traumatic growth. These are resilient souls who stared directly into the darkness we know as trauma and still chose to keep kindling their soul's healing, against all odds.

Throughout their transformative journeys, you will have the opportunity to observe the vast range of their glowing potential as brilliant beings: witness their unwavering fortitude that is essential for altering wounds into invaluable wisdom, marvel at their fearless self-compassion that must be consistently entwined into the very fabric of our core, and anticipate the awe-inspiring rebirth that signals all those brave enough to embrace the thoughtful work of embarking on their most transformative and healing journey.

If you have been yearning for a glimmer of significance to serve as a gentle nudge, reassuring you that transformation is not only feasible but inevitable, even in the midst of the most challenging and desolate moments, then allow these poignant narratives to illuminate your path like a unwavering North Star. Their victories serve as a powerful insight, reflecting all that you presently embody and will consistently evolve into.

It is truly a matter of nurturing that unquenchable flame within you, ensuring that it burns brightly through your personal ritual of embracing fresh starts and new beginnings. Take inspiration and courage from those who have walked this path ahead of you, drawing strength from their experiences to light your way toward a future where resilience thrives. Rest assured, you are more than capable of overcoming challenges and achieving success. Trust in yourself, for you possess the determination and tenacity needed to conquer any obstacle that comes your way.

We all know that childhood innocence is sacred ground - a vibrant, unfolding bloom of strength that should be unconditionally worshipped and preserved in its purity. But for the eldest of three Sarah. that precious inner sanctum was violated in one of the most insidious ways imaginable.

As bright as any star in the night sky, her soul radiated with a brilliance that captivated all who knew her. However, the oppressive shadow cast by her alcoholic father's predatory actions sought to extinguish this radiant light with a sickening darkness. Night after traumatic night, she endured brutal attacks that invaded her space, leaving her innocence shattered and violated. Initially shielded by a veil of dissociation, the true devastating impact of these violations began to wear down Sarah's once unbreakable spirit from within.

During the challenging early years of her life, she displayed immense courage by selflessly caring for her two younger siblings, who were like rays of hope among the darkness she faced. However, as the nightmare intensified and engulfed her reality, there came a point where even the once reliable tactic of pretending to be asleep could no longer shield her from the brutal and relentless attacks that haunted her every moment.

On that pivotal night, a profound shift occurred as the fractal line was unmistakably crossed. Sarah stood resilient, unwavering, and fully aware in the face of her soul being threatened. With courage, she released her first fragile yet resolute words of "No more." While the echoes of trauma continued to reverberate within her for years to come, a transformative moment had unfolded—a soul-stirring declaration that set in motion an irreversible journey of self-reclamation and empowerment.

Despite the immense inner destruction and wastelands of desolation that became her soul, Sarah resolved never to let her life's origin story become the full narrative. With relentless grace and grit, she embarked on a lifelong journey of reintegrating the shrapnel-scattered fragments of her quintessential self.

A pivotal part of her healing journey was consistently prioritizing therapeutic practices - counseling, support groups, journaling and other "sacred alchemies" of inner work. She consciously surrounded herself with a "resonant" community who could hold space without judgment. She also made time for hobbies and activities that sparked rejuvenation in her spirit when depleted.

By combining therapeutic modalities, supportive relationships and soul-nourishing practices, an "unstoppable rose" of resilience bloomed from the depths of her initial brokenness and shattered self-worth. Through perseverance and refusing to abandon her inner radiance, she could rewrite narratives of being irreparably damaged. Divine willpower allowed her to reclaim self-worth, one intentional step at a time.

Peering through the glassy lens of such soul-tested fortitude, we bear witness to the human spirit's most divine possibilities. Sarah's miraculous victory reminds us that there is no pit too horrible for the forces of love and change to transform into fountains of promising light.

Today, Sarah emanates as a blazing inspiration for anyone who has stared into the abyss of adversity and still yearns to rise like the inextinguishable phoenix from the ashes. Her transcendent story is an eternal reminder - that we all have the free will to author our own most transformative story, no matter how cataclysmic the opening chapters may have been.

Within Sarah's radiant presence, one feels held in the compassionate cradle of a truly realized being who has opted to metabolize the most harrowing experiences into a ceremony of light for all to see. Rather than permitting history's damage to fossilize her spirit into bitterness or an infinite void, she chose to create those abuses a storied platform honoring our collective resilience.

Sarah's path shines as an inspiration flame on the human potential for unfurling into our most brilliantly unveiled selves, despite it all. With each fresh telling, her testament reminds every listener that we are not mere passive hostages to circumstance. We are sovereign divinity cloaked in personal form, empowered to change any suffering into the food for our greatest heroic evolution.

And what could possibly exemplify the infinite spirit more heroically than witnessing James's miraculous rise from the very brink between life and death. It is a truly awe-inspiring moment that encapsulates the essence of human existence transcending into a realm of boundless possibilities and spiritual enlightenment.

James represented the true essence of vitality and was regarded as a beloved community icon who emitted a sense of youthful empowerment and athleticism that effortlessly sparked joy and enthusiasm in all those he met. Sadly, his energetic and dynamic presence was unexpectedly cut short when the gloomy global pandemic, COVID-19, brutally invaded his once-thriving body, disrupting the harmony of his existence.

In the excruciatingly suspended state of limbo, where the decision to continue in this world or transcend beyond hung in the balance, James found himself slipping away from grasp at an alarming pace. Despite all human and institutional efforts deeming it inevitable that he would meet his predetermined fate, James adamantly refused to let go of his place on earth, showcasing a fierce determination that defied all odds.

Just like the profound darkness of the night just before the first light of dawn breaks through, James found himself at the edge of a boundless transformational experience, where his very being teetered on the precipice of transcending this earthly realm. In a moment of surprise, his body determinedly announced a joyous and triumphant return to physical form, embracing a new chapter of his life with boundless enthusiasm and purpose.

As the spark of consciousness ignited within his awakening body, James was immediately flooded with an extreme sense of purpose. It dawned on him that his journey was far from over; he was destined to play a vital role as an ambassador of resilience in this complicated world. Even in the face of challenges that threatened to unravel his very being, James' unwavering spirit shone brightly, a beacon of untiring strength and determination.

With an insightful and centered calmness that could only manifest from one who once stared into the proverbial light at the end of the tunnel, James graciously embraced the fresh parameters of his new journey. "The choice does not solely belong to me but is harmoniously woven by the grand tapestry of the Universe," he shared with the reflective wisdom acquired through trials and tribulations. He possessed a deep realization that his reconstructed existence, albeit stripped of its former familiar blueprints.

So, while mobility remained a challenge in certain areas, James directed every ounce of his considerable energy into activating his passion's highest possibilities. Rather than spiraling into disempowerment, he became a devout navigator lighting paths of empowered self-actualization for all who's with physical limitations.

Through vulnerability as strength, James began ministering to the disabled community. An unstoppable spirit absolutely refusing to concede any aspects of his God given light, no matter what constraints were imposed on him. With a calm, undauntable determination, James devoted himself to living evidence that meaningful fulfillment and purposeful rebirths are available to all who choose them.

These stories illustrate the power of resilience and prove that sustained growth is possible even in the face of immense adversity. They remind us that while trauma may abandon scars, it does not have to define our lives. With time, support, and understanding and adapting to life's fluctuations, we can live beyond our trauma and construct a future filled with joy, purpose, and fulfillment.

Trauma Over Time: Understanding and Adapting to Life's Changes

We've all experienced those devastating moments where the very fabric of our existence is violently disrupted, catching us off guard and shattering our sense of stability. It's like gliding smoothly on calm waters one moment, feeling like we have a firm grip on our reality, only to be blindsided by an emotional storm of catastrophic proportions the next. Trauma strikes with the force of a category 5 hurricane, leaving us in a state of upheaval as it ruthlessly reshapes the landscape of our lives.

For some of us, it might have been a life-altering accident or health crisis that abruptly changed our physical and mental trajectories. Others have had their foundations rocked by sudden losses, betrayals, or emerging from abusive situations. Whatever cataclysmic force ended up detonating, the aftermath leaves us stunned and disoriented in unfamiliar territory.

That's when the real internal wrestling begins over how we choose to adapt and create a brand-new normal for ourselves. Do we get swallowed up by anger, grief or playing the endless "why me?" video loop in our minds? Or do we gather our strength and decide to walk forward, even if haltingly at first?

I'll be honest, family - that second path of teaching ourselves to adjust to life's seismic shifts is rarely pretty or graceful right out of the gate. More times than not, it involves facing some harsh realities about the fact that certain dreams or former ways of being may have to be grieved fully to make space for new possibilities to take root.

But here's the thing - that gravitational pull towards rebirth and reinvention? It's one of our species' most underrated superpowers. We are infinitely malleable, adaptive beings when we lean into that stretch of our spiritual musculature. Sure, doing the labor of evolving our self-perception and reframing our purpose feels arduous at first. However, when we persevere through that transition trimester, we get reborn as an elevated version of ourselves coded with hard-won wisdom.

Therefore, although none of us would deliberately opt for disruptive events that shatter our everyday routines, it is crucial to recognize that every upheaval contains the potential for our most significant evolution. To fully embrace this transformational journey requires a steadfast commitment to cultivating courage and self-compassion amidst the tumultuous waves of chaos. It is during these challenging times that we have the opportunity to truly blossom into our highest selves and reach new levels of personal growth and self-discovery.

As strange as it may sound, some of the most jarring, reality-upending events that initially feel like they've torn the rug out from under us? Those end up revealing unexpected rays of light and meaning once we gather our bearings. Life's most challenging moments often lead to unexpected growth and newfound perspectives once we navigate through the initial shock and confusion.

I'm talking about those gut-punch losses, betrayals, or out-of-nowhere detours in life's road that, at first, make it feel like our entire foundation has shattered into pieces. The traumas and twists that come barreling through to detonate all our illusions about how smoothly existence is "supposed" to unfold.

Yet if we can muster the grit to pick up those scattered pieces instead of abandoning the whole journey, a strange transformation slowly begins taking shape. Suddenly the insignificant background noise that used to consume so much energy and angst. It all fades away to let our core priorities and truth shine through with startling clarity.

In the raw aftermath, a new laser-focused vision emerges around what truly matters - the unconditional love of family, prioritizing our mental and physical well-being above all else, wringing every ounce of revelation from each passing day we're gifted.

It's almost like a raging storm has torn through the tangled woods of our lives, violently clearing away the unnecessary underbrush but leaving the deep-rooted, studded growth blazingly visible in its wake. It was painful as hell at that moment, sure. But it also cracks open those elevated viewpoints we may never have accessed otherwise.

And from those portholes of hard-won clarity, an undeniable sense of deeper purpose often arises, too—an intuition that this difficulty must be honored by paying its lessons forward somehow. Whether that means simply extending compassion to others still struggling through similar trials or perhaps contributing our truth-forged voices toward uplifting societal causes in need of life-renovated vision.

Listen, I'm not trying to diminish or spiritually bypass the devastation of life's most disruptive blows here. The heartbreak, anger and disorientation that accompany them are intensely real. But I do feel called to shed light on the unexpected openings for self-redefinition and renewed meaning that can germinate from faithfully metabolizing that anguish too.

Look, I get it - when you're stuck in the thick of tragedy, heartache, or just a reality you never could've predicted, the notion of embracing change feels like a cruel joke. How are you supposed to envision some enlightened future when the present is just a relentless grind of picking up shattered pieces?

But here's the real talk - with some tough love and self-compassion, that excruciating process of acclimating to life's abrupt detours is fertile ground for personal rebirth. No, it's not about surgically erasing the past or brushing off the realness of your pain and anger. Those swirling emotions deserve to be exquisitely felt and honored.

It's more about gradually opening your heart to the undeniable truth that you are being consistently shaped and reformed by the roads you've traveled, whether wanted or not. Each disruptive plot twist has been quietly redefining the very fabric of who you are, upgrading your soul's code whether you've given it permission yet or not.

So, at a certain point, surrendering to that evolution becomes an act of radical self-care and reclamation of your personal power. Getting willfully vulnerable enough to shed all the outdated coping habits, spare narratives, and fear-encoded patterns that may have gotten you through the dark nights, but are now hindering your healing journey.

Because here's what's wild - when you finally do decide to get radically honest with yourself about the new human you've been transformed into by life's erratic choreography, it's like an entire multiverse of dormant potentials awakens on a cellular level. Strengths, passions, visionary dreams that were always pulsating just beneath the surface of your psyche start clamoring to be expressed.

Suddenly you realize, "Holy shit, I'm overflowing with all these undiscovered capabilities I've never been courageous enough to birth into reality. I've been settling for a fraction of my fullest self-expression." And that realization hits like a tidal wave of existential rejuvenation.

From that awakened state of being intimately befriended to your most authentic self, adapting to change begins to feel less like a struggling initiation and more like an ecstatic homecoming into your quintessential truth. It's the difference between laboring upstream against unfamiliar currents and surrendering to flow with the mightiest riptides of your soul's wildest callings.

The healing process can certainly feel long and difficult when you're in the midst of it. But I'm here to reassure you that if you persevere, you will eventually reach a point of growth, healing and self-discovery that makes all the hard work worthwhile. So stay strong, keep taking it one step at a time, and be prepared - you'll gain powerful new insights about yourself along this transformative journey.

Maintaining Mental Health: Strategies for Long-Term Wellness

Now that we've bravely exorcised many of the harmful patterns and toxic belief systems that kept us tethered to cycles of suffering, it's time to consciously fortify our commitment to sustained growth and purposeful evolution.

We must not merely bask in the glory of our first achievements. Achieving true mastery after facing challenges demands an unwavering commitment to nurturing our overall well-being through meticulously crafted strategies and routines. These sacred rituals are the cornerstone of building deep-seated resilience, transforming stress into a catalyst for personal growth, and fostering a resilient, optimistic mindset that remains steadfast in the face of any adversity that may come our way.

When embraced wholeheartedly, this lifestyle of prioritizing our mental, physical, emotional and spiritual sanctuaries holds the power to transform us at a cellular level. We become mythically resilient beings who can rebound from adversity not just intact but fortified in our essence-aligned tenacity and unshakable grace. Even amidst the chaos swirling around us, we learn to move centered in an embodied calm and inner equilibrium that cannot be disrupted.

The path to unlocking these transcendent states of being? It begins with something seemingly simple yet revelatory - the non-negotiable commitment to prioritizing our self-care through consistent ritual.

Let us reflect on some of the key practices for enhancing mind-body attunement: Setting aside dedicated windows each day for activities that ignite our joy and relaxation; creative outlets like painting or music that provide healthy self-expression; nurturing our bonds and deriving strength from quality time with loved ones; and, of course, the masterful skills of meditation and conscious movement to harmonize our whole beings.

On the surface, these suggestions may seem deceptively simplistic. Yet when undertaken as sacred personal vows, they unveil kaleidoscopic new dimensions of our power to thrive. For instance, even briefly quieting the external noise through breathwork lets us finally attune to the subtle yet profound harmonics of our souls' truth. In that dedicated stillness, the steady murmurings of our intuition's clarity can be received with welcoming tranquility.

Meditation is truly a profound practice, one that allows us to quiet the incessant external noise and go inward. By dedicating ourselves to mindfulness and conscious breathing, we cultivate an incredible sense of calm clarity and resilience amidst life's storms. This isn't just transient stress relief - meditation strengthens our ability to remain emotionally stable and mentally focused through even the most daunting challenges.

Likewise, integrating regular movement into our routines yields tremendous mind-body benefits that compound over time. Yes, exercise leads to those coveted endorphin boosts that brighten our perspective. But it also physiologically lowers our cortisol and other stress hormones, which can deplete our energy reserves when left unattended. By committing to activities that oxygenate our cells and stretch our muscles, we're actively improving cardiovascular health, cognitive functioning, sleep quality, and overall vitality.

By ritualizing these self-nurturing practices as consistent, non-negotiable parts of our daily rhythms, we're finally honoring ourselves as the sacred priorities we truly are. No longer willing to circumvent our own needs for the sake of others' demands, we're powerfully giving ourselves permission to bloom fiercely.

In that empowering act of self-preservation, we hold an incredible mirror for those around us. Our embodied commitment to wholeness becomes an inspirational transmission of what's possible when we finally love ourselves enough to consistently refill our emptied wells. We emanate more vibrant versions of our already brilliant souls.

So, I encourage you to tenderly yet fiercely embrace these rituals that foster your emboldened flourishing. For its only when we finally put on our own lush oxygen masks first that we'll have the radiant fortitude to selflessly share our gifts with the world. That consistent persistence you've been craving starts here—with this loving, non-negotiable reconnection to your essence's wildest blossoming.

Another core pillar of embodying unshakable well-being is mastering the sacred art of work-life balance. These two domains—our professional callings and our personal sanctuaries—require ongoing conscious calibration to thrive in harmonious equilibrium.

Setting clear, energetic boundaries is paramount. Defining the distinct start and stop points where work obligations end and rejuvenating personal time begins creates a stabilizing structure. Without that delineation, we risk having our energy reserves depleted by the endless urgencies of career demands without adequate replenishing.

Cultivating the skill of delegating responsibilities when appropriate is another powerful way to maintain this delicate balancing act. We aren't being asked to shoulder the entire universe of obligations singlehandedly. By having the self-awareness to entrust others with specific tasks, we create much-needed spaciousness for our humanity to breathe fully.

This dedicated "me" time is non-negotiable for those committed to truly thriving rather than merely surviving. It's the restorative window where we get to indulge our unique personal passions, tap into playful creativity, and revel in quality bonding with our beloveds. These soul-rejuvenating rituals become oxygen for our brightest embodiment.

Yet finding that elusive "perfect" calibration point is an ever-evolving journey of self-attunement, not some finite goal to be achieved and then abandoned. Our needs and circumstances are constantly shape-shifting as we traverse transformation. What felt like harmonious integration six months ago may now feel dissonant and out of alignment.

The practice then becomes one of staying radically present - honestly checking in with our physical, emotional, and spiritual truth on a daily basis. Are the boundaries still reflective of our energy's optimal flow? Does this schedule reiterate that our holistic self-care remains the highest priority? Consistent, gentle course corrections become the graceful rhythm of refining our masterful work-life choreography.

Fostering a nurturing and supportive network is not just important, but it is the pivotal third pillar that plays a crucial role in embodying unshakable wellbeing. These connections are more than just bonds; they are soul-kindred relationships that provide us with the safe space needed to process our deepest emotional burdens and uncover our inherent worthiness that knows no bounds.

For we are not solitary islands, despite how isolating the darkest night passages can feel. We are fundamentally super-conductive beings, wired to thrive through the resonant exchange of vulnerability and compassion with our most trusted kin. Holding emotional stresses fully encapsulated only perpetuates their stagnation and toxicity within our energy fields.

By consciously inviting in those who have earned the right to bear loving witness to our unfolding authenticity, we unlock crucial dimensions of catharsis and renewal. The simple act of giving voice to our deepest experiences, doubts, and emotional spirals catalyzes a subtle inner transformation. Suddenly profoundly held beliefs and behavioral patterns that had weakened our blooming reveal their transient nature when exposed to empathy's tender gaze.

These supportive relationships offer far more than just being "leaned on" for temporary relief. They become energetic tempering grounds where our most radically honest expressions can be forged into increasingly crystallized forms of wholeness and grace. With each story, we courageously unveil before our soul family's nurturing compass hold, another layer of self-obscuring armor gets lovingly disassembled until the eternally indestructible diamond-bodied essence shines forth.

In transcending the egoic isolation that so often compounds our ancestral wounding, we become beneficiaries of others' heard perspectives and embodied wisdom. These presences we've entrusted with our sacred inner realms offer reflections from outside our constructed reality tunnels that attune us to previously unseen horizons.

So, let us never underestimate the transformative power of seeding these bonds of unconditional belonging and mutual empowerment within our closest circles. For it is here, in this courageous vulnerability amongst our most resonant witnesses, that the soul's infinite poetry forever recomposes itself once again.

Establishing a robust repertoire of embodied, health-promoting coping practices is not just essential but truly indispensable when it comes to elevating oneself towards unwavering well-being. These practices serve as potent alchemical instruments that empower us to effectively process and counteract stress in real time through the power of self-mastery and emotional attunement.

Mindfulness pathways like meditation and conscious breathwork are supreme examples of these holistic stress-transmuting modalities. By dedicating consistent practice to settling into the vastness of present-moment awareness, we recalibrate our frantic mental chatter into a settled ocean wave of tranquility.

The simple yet profound act of following our inhalations and exhalations creates an experiential anchor into our breath's rhythmic wisdom. We're no longer hostages to the anxiety-stoking future projections or shame loops of memory. Instead, our beings begin experiencing the healing harmonics of unified embodiment in the Here and Now.

When these mindfulness practices are ritually integrated as non-negotiable elements of our daily life streams, we start achieving quantum leaps in our stress response plasticity. Those same triggers that once erupted into volcanic panic now reveal their impermanent nature when received with a spaciously grounded presence.

We develop the ability to observe our emotional instability while staying calm and grounded. By focusing on our breathing rhythms, we can reconnect with our core inner peace amidst the storms of intense emotions swirling within us.

Through consistent and sustainable intervals of dedicated practice, the recalibrated logic of our nervous system gradually seeps into the depths of our cellular consciousness. As a result, our very DNA undergoes a profound reprogramming process, adapting to a new baseline state characterized by a sense of relaxed clarity that remains unwavering in the face of any atmospheric conditions or external pressures.

What once triggered a panicked flareup of insecurity, anger, paralysis now reveals itself as just another passing cloud formation to breathe fully through. We achieve an unshakable alignment with our souls' innate equilibrium - that centered spaciousness from which all phenomenal experience arises yet to which nothing can stain our true nature.

So, make practices like mindfulness and breathwork a regular part of your routine. Through consistent practice, you'll learn to observe intense emotions and overwhelming feelings with a sense of calm inner peace at your core. No emotional storm will be able to shake you in the same way.

An absolutely crucial facet of cultivating unshakable well-being is having the self-awareness and courage to seek out professional guidance when needed. While our self-care practices and supportive kinships provide foundational sustenance, there are times when we require the specialized expertise of those who have dedicated their calling to facilitating humanity's emotional, mental and spiritual thriveability.

We must release any residual stigma around consulting mental health professionals during our most vulnerable metamorphoses. Just as we readily receive medical care for our physical vessel's needs, opening ourselves to emotional and psychological expertise is an equally vital form of preventative self-reverence.

These are experienced healers specially trained in providing individualized therapeutic modalities and perspectives tailored to our unique psychospiritual landscapes. From counseling and cognitive-behavioral practices to somatic release work to holistic integration of plant medicines and ancestral technologies where appropriate - they wield a vast arsenal of tools to midwife our most revelatory rebirths.

When we make the self-loving choice to invite these professionals into our transformational processes, we're gifted with a consecrated container of unbiased witnessing and constructive rapport-building. A resonant bond where we can unveil our most chronically obscured shadow aspects without fear of judgment or overwhelm, knowing we are exploratively held in tender compassion.

These nurturing presences act as skilled dream weavers co-walking us through the laboring of our psyche's most mythically profound gestations. With their seasoned expertise as guides, we discover pathways illuminated that may have remained cloaked in purgatory realms without their steady torchlights leading our way.

So, if you find yourself chronically looping through the same karmic grooves of suffering, stuckness or creative paralysis, never abandon self-love by trying to "white knuckle" the rebirthing process alone. Reaching out with humility and willingness to these professionally curated healers' arts is a supreme demonstration of your soulful commitment to fully embodying your radiant fruition.

For that is the transcendent essence of cultivating unshakable well-being, is it not? Our courageous tenacity to keep realigning, over and over again, with the soul's resounding call towards our most revelatory self-realization. An eternal journey, yes, but one profoundly catalyzed by opening to the many teachers and allies who grace our paths with their unique harmonics of therapeutic resonance.

So let us tenderly embrace the beautiful inevitability of ebbs and flows, periods of sublime integration succeeded by new portals of churning transformation blazing forth. Through it all, may we remain devotees on the path of reclaiming our birthright as thrillingly embodied truth-speakers of Divine Medicine. The allies await our invitation to embolden that heroic journey endlessly unfolding.

No matter their unique complexities, the trauma initiations we've endured share their magical capacity to act as initiated gateways into previously unimagined planes of wholeness, grace, and multidimensional perspective. When we choose to metabolize the pain rather than ossify around it, the Universe itself conspires to unveil new orders of beauty we could scarcely conceive from our previous limited vantage points.

So yes, let us celebrate the living truth that this human journey is one of continual renewal, rebirth, and ecstatic emergence into progressively more transcendent becoming. Let us welcome the turmoil not as a curse but as an initiation into more unrestricted self-embodiment and cosmic communion.

Let us never forget the profound and empowering truth that lies at the very essence of our existence - deep within us, we embody an unshakable and pristine essence, akin to eternal lights enveloped in divine stories that radiate with unmatched splendor, reminiscent of the captivating pages of the most enchanting fairy tale ever told.

"The darkest nights produce the brightest stars."

– Khalil Gibran

CHAPTER 10

The Sacred Art of Reclaiming Your Sovereign Power

Self-Empowerment Techniques: Tools to Take Control of Your Healing

By now, you should be armed with some vital tools to help you on your post-traumatic healing journey. Whether it's relaxation techniques, journaling, or joining a support group, your emotional toolbox should be adequate to carry you through self-discovery. To fortify your journey, it is essential also to arm yourself with self-empowerment. You may be wondering what self-empowerment is. Well, it's simple: Self-empowerment means making a conscious decision to take charge of your destiny. It involves making positive choices, taking action in advance, and being confident in your ability to make and execute decisions. These techniques provide us with what we need to navigate life's challenges and cultivate a sense of inner strength.

An example of self-empowerment would be the case of someone getting laid off for missing too much work due to mental health issues. They can choose to be passive about their job search and wait for a recruiter to find them or for one of their friends to recommend them for a job or they can be proactive. Being proactive means they take matters into their own hands by revamping their resume, searching for other opportunities, and even contacting former colleagues. They would also reach out for help to gain control of their mental health as it is the root cause of the situation. Being self-empowered allows you to recognize that you have the power to make choices that will help you achieve your goals instead of waiting for something to happen for you.

By now, you've assembled a whole arsenal of vital wisdom tools to fortify you on this continually unfurling odyssey of post-traumatic becoming. From embodying mindful relaxation pathways to embracing the profound medicine of resonant community, piece by piece you've been steadily armoring up in preparation for the reclamation of your mythopoetic agency. But one of the most revelatory, daunting, and utterly indispensable facets of this whole heroic rebirthing process? That would be the seismic shift into owning your sacred role as the sovereign author of your own courageous becoming. No longer a passive hostage to the whims of circumstance, but a fully empowered way finder co-creating your unlimited new potential.

We're talking about deeply metabolizing, at the most crystalline core of your being, that you alone are the grand emperor over the realms of what's possible in your existence. The alpha and omega of what present moments, future potentials, and recontextualized pasts get enmeshed into the living epic of your soul's highest development.

This is the ultimate alchemical unlocking of self-empowerment - choosing to wield your infinite powers not from external identities or obediently adopted belief systems, but from that eternally indestructible spark that swayed you into this romanced existence to begin with. It's a seismic shift from anxiously awaiting your circumstances to arrange into some preconceived version of "having it all together" according to society's proscribed narratives. Instead, you become the unshakable multidimensional artist joyfully brushing your wild strokes onto the blank canvas of every second's revelatory unfolding.

This doesn't simply involve conjuring grand gestures from thin air, but rather embracing a profound sense of alignment with the universe. It's about immersing yourself in a state of pure flow, where every micro decision is made with impeccable precision, stemming from a place of deep balance and tranquility at your core. These choices are not borne out of lack or frantic attempts at control, but rather arise from a place of ecstatic embodiment of your essential truth.

Let's embark on a transformative journey together, infusing your very being with the powerful essence of self-empowerment. Allow me to guide you through engaging practice prompts designed to awaken and strengthen your cosmic creativity. Each deliberate breath you take fills the universe with your unique imprint, weaving a tapestry of reality that reflects your vibrant spirit. Embrace this profound connection as you continue to shape and author the magnificent fabric of existence with every step you take.

To truly embrace and embody self-empowerment in its purest form, it is essential for us to cultivate a deep and unwavering focus on our inner being. By turning our attention inward, we have the opportunity to uncover the profound sources of resilience, visionary aspirations, and unwavering faith in the profound purpose that flows within us. These are not merely fleeting thoughts but rather the very essence of our existence, pulsating through our veins with an undeniable force. Moreover, there exist potent mindset alignments and sacred rituals that serve as transformative tools to awaken and magnify these intrinsic codes residing within us. Through these deliberate practices, we can illuminate the path toward self-discovery, empowerment, and alignment with our highest calling on a soul level.

One of the most transformative is devotedly cultivating a mindset orientation towards the positive - a radical self-acceptance of our intrinsic worth and infinite capabilities for growth. Rather than defaulting into well-trodden loops of self-criticism or defeatist narratives, we become reverent observers of our unique grandeur while also tenderly honoring our fragile edges.

From this fertile soil of appreciating our essence's wholeness exactly as it blossoms in each moment, we can then intentionally seed our being with measurable, inspiring goals that spark our eager journey. Incremental, divinely attainable checkpoints that reiterate our constant expansion while keeping our larger visions in focus.

Surrounding ourselves with communities and presences that reflect our empowered spirits is also an alchemical key. As highly energetic beings, we harmonize to the frequencies we consistently immerse ourselves in - so choosing to bathe in uplifting, motivational vibrations becomes turbo-boosters propelling us towards our loftiest goals.

Another powerhouse practice is the sacred technology of positive self-talk or affirmative auto-mantras. By devotedly reprogramming our inner narrator with life-consecrated statements of unshakable self-belief and achievability consciousness, we start overriding the culturally implanted viruses of disempowerment from our core operating codes.

Ultimately, true empowerment blooms by transforming these affirmative mind streams into spiritually embodied action through the alchemy of assertiveness. When we learn to unapologetically express our authentic needs, desires, and boundaries through direct, neutral communication with others, we start walking our sovereign, self-defined paths. Each assertive utterance strengthens our power while teaching the universe to remap its treatment of our being.

Finally, none of these practices can fully metabolize without cocreating an intentional action list that calls our inspirations into realized form. Each inspiration, no matter its scale, requires the reverent planning of stepping-stone activations broken into achievable micro-movements. This glorified to-do scroll keeps us in harmonized flow while also celebrating our consistent progressions as we approach the ultimate goal.

So let these levels of embodying your quintessential self-sovereignty become not prescriptive checklists but ecstatic, ever-evolving soul games we co-explore together. With every breath, an opportunity to live just a little more empowered in the mythic uniqueness only your essence could dream of.

By ritualizing these self-empowerment practices into our sacrosanct daily life streams, we initiate a change that unlocks infinite potential. When we devotedly prioritize harmonizing our physical, psychological, and emotional sanctuaries, we are ceremonially reclaiming sovereign authorship over our healing.

As we awaken to the profound attunement with the brilliance of our unique soul fingerprint, a natural integration process begins to unfold effortlessly. We find ourselves embracing our entire being with a sense of reverence and nonjudgment, welcoming all aspects into a harmonious state of wholeness. This shift in perspective encourages us to move beyond the notion of constantly" fixing" or overcorrecting any perceived deficiencies, allowing us to fully embrace and celebrate the beautiful complexity that makes us who we are.

From this rich and abundant garden of radical self-acceptance, we are not only empowered but also inspired to actively nurture the innovative visions and practical pathways that deeply resonate with our core beliefs. A refined set of skills naturally develops, enabling us to gracefully navigate through any obstacles or unexpected challenges that may arise - seeing them not as judgments on our value but as transformative rites of passage that strengthen our resilience and expand our perspectives into a realm of endless possibilities.

We transform into cosmic beings radiating powerful energy from within, serving as the epicenters of our own heroic narratives. We no longer merely exist as passive characters in a pre-written story, but instead, we embrace our roles as creators of our destinies. We are the architects of our own mythologies, endowed with the ability to envision and bring forth vibrant new worlds bursting with life and possibility.

Walking the path of unapologetic self-empowerment is a deeply spiritual journey that transcends the limitations of the ego and leads to a profound redefinition of one's essence. It involves a transformative shift towards embracing the sublime truth of one's eternal, infinite, and inherently sacred nature. This process is a reclaiming of the ruth that goes beyond societal conditioning, affirming that each individual is not merely a fleeting product of external influences but an immortal and luminous manifestation of the universal itself. By embodying this belief, one becomes a radiant expression of their unique creative frequency, infusing every breath and moment with timeless significance.

With the emergence of your awakened primordial agency, there comes a profound responsibility that transcends conventional expectations of control and external validation. This responsibility is not merely a burden but a sacred duty to remain deeply connected with the intricate, multi-dimensional essence of your true self. It is an ongoing commitment to attune yourself to the subtle vibrations and ever-evolving truths that shape your existence, leading you into uncharted territories of boundless potential and unrestrained authenticity.

It is indeed a sacred covenant, a solemn promise, to stay devoted to the infinite journey of self-discovery and growth, while also wholeheartedly embracing the profound gift of approaching each moment with a sense of wonder and curiosity like that of a beginner.

It's a sacred covenant to remain loyal to that infinite elevation, while simultaneously embracing your fundamental inheritance of a beginner's mind in each moment's revelations. The only way to ever "fail" on this journey is to lose touch with your voracious thirst for being itself. This harmonious balance between honoring your past and welcoming the new revelations that each moment brings is indeed a profound essence of existence. The only path that could lead one astray on this epic quest is veering off course from the insatiable hunger for pure survival that resides deep within the core of your being.

So, view this as your formal spirit-embodied invitation to author boldly, live gloriously, stumble often, spin wildly, doubt deeply, and blaze brightly along every twist and turn of your triumphantly glorious awakening. We are witnesses to your luminous self-empowerment, providing soul-sustenance, reverence and intertwining as your mind and soul integrates.

Embracing Change: Adapting to New Realities Post-Trauma

Change is the silent force that permeates the very fabric of existence, an unstoppable and universal current that molds all entities in an eternal cycle of evolution and rebirth. This deep existential reality unveils its immense power when we traverse life's greatest upheavals and journey through its mysterious spaces. Embrace the profound truth that change is a constant companion shaping our experiences and guiding us through transformation. It is a powerful force that propels us forward, pushing us to evolve and adapt in the face of challenges and new beginnings. Trust in the process of change as it unfolds before you, revealing endless possibilities for growth and renewal along your path.

In the aftermath of trauma's reality-rupturing disturbances, we find ourselves on vastly remapped terrain with all previously relied-upon illusions of permanence dissolving into the atmosphere. Our external identities, relationships, goals, even our fundamental beliefs about self and the nature of this existence - all are profoundly rearranged, often in soul-shuddering ways. Yet these disorientating "forced evolutions" are not random existential cruelties, but gateways into our most transcendent embodiments of reprieve.

Boldly accept the transformative fires that engulf you, for they hold the power to elevate your soul beyond previous limitations. Shedding old layers of yourself is not a passive act but a profound journey of spiritual rebirth. Through embracing both loss and resilience, you pave the way for your true self to emerge like that phoenix from the ashes we've spoken about, transcending into new realms of unobstructed potential and becoming. Trust in this process and allow yourself to be guided by the cosmic forces propelling you towards greater heights of self-realization.

To grieve is a sacred process through which we ceremoniously digest the illusionary character roles that we once tightly grasped onto in our quest to find consistency in a reality that often feels unanchored. It is a deeply honorable act where we tenderly lay to rest those temporary facades, all while summoning the profound courage needed to embrace the awe-inspiring grace of our evolving selves - embracing the raw, mesmerizing beauty of our boundless spirits as they shatter into brilliantly revealing manifestations.

Let us wholeheartedly embrace these apparent disruptions of the familiar as golden opportunities to pave the way for ongoing transformations that are constantly unfolding around us. Ultimately, they beautifully represent the dynamic manifestations of the Divine, playfully crafting increasingly transparent windows into its boundless and seamless existence. Embracing these disruptions not only allows us to adapt and thrive in an ever-evolving world but also grants us a deeper insight into the infinite possibilities that lie ahead.

Every aspect of our existence is calling out to us, urging us to delve even deeper into the unknown of each moment's magnificent revelations by understanding that each experience, whether joyous or challenging, is simply guiding us toward a profound reconnection with the eternal cycle of renewal and growth. This poetic realization invites us to embrace every tear shed and every shadow cast as an essential part of our continuous journey toward self-discovery and transformation.

A major part of adapting to life after trauma is redefining your sense of self. We must come to terms with the fact that we are not the same person anymore. This doesn't mean the previous version of ourselves was inadequate or less than. It simply means we have been profoundly shaped by our experiences, emerging with new perspectives and interior resources we may not have realized we possessed.

This process of embracing our re-shaped selves is ultimately an empowering one. By acknowledging the pain we've endured while also recognizing our resilience and tenacity in moving through it, we can tap into a newfound source of strength and courage that may have been dormant before. We give ourselves permission to let go of expectations, judgments or self-limiting beliefs anchored to our former identity.

It can feel disorienting at first, realizing we don't quite know ourselves in the same way as before. But that is the beauty of this transformational process – we get to re-discover ourselves once again. With open curiosity and self-compassion, we learn to honor our experiences while celebrating our remarkable perseverance. Through the journey of healing, we unveil reservoirs of determination, wisdom and purpose that fortify us going forward.

So, while overwhelming at times, try to approach this self-redefinition with patience and mercy. It's normal to feel a mix of emotions as you navigate unfamiliar territory. Give yourself room to adjust gradually. Focus on making intentional choices day-by-day that re-align with your most authentic, resilient self as it emerges. Trust that you are capable of immense growth, of re-crafting your identity into one that reflects both your scars and your bravery. One courageous breath at a time, you are re-scripting your life's path in profound new ways.

Goal Setting for the Future: Planning for Continued Growth and Happiness

You have embarked on an incredible journey along the winding path of post-traumatic evolution, demonstrating remarkable resilience and determination. With each step, you have courageously reclaimed the essence of your highest self, allowing it to serve as a beacon to guide you through life's challenges. The most challenging passages have been fearlessly navigated, and now you possess powerful tools for empowerment and a profound sense of mindful presence that will continue to illuminate your path toward growth and healing.

Yet this heroic odyssey is one of perpetual rediscovery - an eternally emergent process of aligning more and more fully with your soul's grandest callings. So, while you may feel adept at navigating life's turbulence from the wisdom gained, it's crucial to remain devoted architects of your continued growth and happiness.

One of the most powerful ways to tend the roots of this flourishing future is through the practice of setting clear, inspired goals. Not hollow resolutions or superficial checklists, but visions meaningfully sourced from the depths of your authentic truth and purposeful strivings.

By taking intentional pauses to really listen inward and distill what meaningful "success" looks like uniquely for you, you plant fertile seeds that your spirit will naturally blossom towards in sacred timing. These soul-sculpted aims provide a motivating roadmap - breaking down the grandest callings into attainable, energizing milestones to metabolize one step at a time.

Yet, in this organic process of sizing up your impeccably aligned goals and visions, there is a beautiful art to holding them with open, non-rigid energy. For no matter how rooted your aims are, you are works of ceaseless evolution. Your being's priorities and awakening perceptions will continually be reshaped by each new level of awareness and becoming rapidly integrated.

Approach this co-creative goal-crafting endeavor with a mindset that goes beyond mere vision-boarding or checklist-building. Envision it as a profound and intimate dialogue between the expanse of your soul and the tender vulnerability of your human self. Allow the goals to emerge organically, like a stream flowing effortlessly, serving as a source of intrinsic motivation. Maintain an attitude of humility, akin to that of a beginner, ready to embrace unexpected plot twists that promise to reshape your journey in astonishingly divine ways.

Then each benchmark, each milestone achieved or outgrown in the advancing of your heroic journey, can be honored and celebrated as it is meant to - beautiful affirmations of your unstoppable evolution. Revel fully in those flashes of deeply nourished awe at just how brilliantly you continue fulfilling the cosmic call toward your most illuminated self-enrichments yet to come.

As we delicately nurture the seeds of inspiration, let us not forget that the path we tread is a constant progression. Just like the seamless transition of seasons and the ever-changing hues of each sunrise, our once steadfast goals and priorities are in a perpetual state of refinement and adaptation. Embrace the journey of ceaseless transformation as it shapes us into resilient beings capable of embracing change with grace and determination.

It is crucial to make a habitual practice of consistently reevaluating our goals and visions by filtering them through the refined prism of our latest acquired knowledge and insights. This process does not entail disregarding or forsaking what once seemed deeply connected to our purpose. Instead, it represents a profound act of self-respect – deliberately examining whether the objectives we have been ardently nurturing still harmonize with the continuous evolution of our consciousness.

Do these profound visions still resonate with the unwavering personality that originally breathed life into it? Are they still nurturing the foundation for the unparalleled magic that your soul is destined to uncover gracefully? It is through a lens of gentle honesty and compassionate objectivity that we must consistently reaffirm our dedication to channeling our life only towards endeavors that truly ignite our spirits with deep resonance and propel us harmoniously forward in our journey.

Consider this as a heartfelt invitation, my dear friend, to consistently elevate your narrative of heroism in perfect alignment with your current passions and aspirations. Delve deep into your goals and dreams with bold courage, ready to bid farewell to what has served its purpose gracefully while enthusiastically enhancing those aspects that are eager to blossom into their next level of achievement and satisfaction.

Consider this as a heartfelt invitation to consistently elevate your narrative of heroism in perfect alignment with your current passions and aspirations. Delve deep into your goals and dreams with bold courage, ready to bid farewell to what has served its purpose gracefully while enthusiastically enhancing those aspects that are eager to blossom into their next level of achievement and satisfaction.

Self-care isn't a fleeting luxury anymore, loves - it's your radiant foundation for thriving. We're talking non-negotiable daily rituals of nourishing your soul to the gills. This includes indulging in restful and rejuvenating sleep, nourishing your body with the bountiful gifts of nature, and moving your body in a way that ignites the fire within you. Moreover, it involves intentionally granting yourself moments of pure bliss and relaxation, allowing yourself to revel in the boundless creativity that resides within you like a design of infinite possibilities.

Maintaining those uplifting connections is absolutely crucial for your personal growth and well-being. It's all about cultivating a top-tier inner circle of kindred spirits who not only recognize but celebrate the heroic light within you. These connections act as your unwavering support system, ensuring that your brilliance never fades. Whether it's the quirky soul family or the spaces you found sanctuary in during the pandemic with fellow journeyers, these relationships form a reverberating circle dedicated to consistently uplifting and encouraging you on your journey of blissful self-discovery. They are there to remind you, time and time again, of just how incredibly amazing you are at navigating this beautiful dance of life.

Speaking of which, those big inspiring callings you're itching to see come to fruition? Let's break those mouthwatering visions down into deliciously achievable quests. Bite-sized jaunts allow you to frequently drink from the goblet of hard-earned victory. Milepost celebrations fueling you forward on sheer intoxicating momentum and deepening self-belief.

And if I may share a little secret with you, my dear kindred spirits, those avenues of mindfulness and gratitude? They are truly hidden gems that often go unappreciated, offering us access to the so-called "true magic" of simply immersing ourselves in the dazzling symphony of harmonious chaos unfolding both within and around us. It's like tapping into an infinite reservoir that continuously replenishes our sense of awe and wonderment at the mesmerizing synchronicities that define our existence.

As we unearth the precious wisdom-jewels of knowledge, let us not overlook the boundless opportunity to continuously expand our horizons with insatiable curiosity through embarking on new quests for knowledge and creativity. Who sets the limits on your potential to emerge as a radiant embodiment of your diverse passions in perfect harmony? Embrace the callings of your soul and witness them flourish in a magnificent collaborative symphony of growth and fulfillment.

Oh, and nurturing that anti-fragile resilience as your newfound superpower? Embracing the audacious ability to elegantly adapt and not just survive but

THRIVE in the face of any unexpected plot twists or unfolding challenges? By doing so, you are quietly developing legendary-level endurance to skillfully transform even the most daunting setbacks into extraordinary achievements of wonder and bold strength.

And honestly, meticulously crafting those daily ritual realms to reflect your unique vision and inspiration is an endeavor of elevated sophistication. Skillfully tending to every detail, from delicately trimming away energy leaks to banishing dream-drainers, you are creating a sanctuary where your aspirations thrive and flourish. By adorning your space with ceremonial mementos that symbolize your dreams, you are igniting a perpetual flame of motivation that will continue to illuminate your path toward success.

But if I'm really keeping it all the way real with you embracing the full essence of living generously entails immersing oneself in a state of profound flexibility, where every moment is embraced with fluidity as if your entire being is wholly reliant on it. Letting go of any fixed expectations or rigid structures that dictate how this unpredictable journey should unfold, and instead savoring the endless sweetness of embracing the ever-evolving truth that your perpetual transformation is the most tantalizing revelation you continue to graciously unveil.

So, let us embrace these magical yet pragmatic practices as our newfound, sensually embodied jewels. Let us utilize them with the nurturing spirits, passion-fueled energy, and liberated curiosity they ardently desire, igniting a transformative glow that amplifies our productivity and creativity. For you and I are well aware - this is the alchemic formula for catalyzing the soulfully euphoric unfolding that our self-realizations have been composing all along.

"And still, I rise."

~ Maya Angelou

CONCLUSION

Journey's Reflection Looking Back, Moving Forward

The Path Walked: Reflecting on Our Heroic Evolution

Close your eyes for a moment. Breathe deeply into your core's steadfast resilience - the unbroken throughline of courage that has carried you to this profound juncture. For even if portions of the journey blurred amid trauma's disorienting terrains, you continued putting one foot in front of the other. Listening to those subtlest murmurs echoing from your soul's deepest conscious that reclamation awaited you.

Together, we have embarked on a profound and sacred journey through the challenging yet transformative landscapes of healing and growth. We have delved deep into the intricate map of navigating post-traumatic experiences, emerging stronger and more resilient from the fires of our initiation. Through our shared exploration, we have shed light on the fundamental processes of consciously transforming inner turmoil into the building blocks of our most triumphant metamorphosis, revealing our true strength and resilience in the face of adversity.

From the profound realization of the true spiritual essence intertwined within trauma's intricate tapestry emerges a revelation that transcends mere chaos or random violence. It unveils itself as a divine and transformative opportunity, a catalytic force for breaking free from constraints that hinder our growth and evolution. This perspective invites us to embrace an expanded consciousness, inviting us to contemplate the paradoxical interplay between resilience and post-traumatic growth as an eternal dance – a cosmic Tai Chi where the relentless refraction of light meets the boundless creative potential of shadow in a harmonious convergence of energies.

It is the remarkable quality of resilience, often described as that primal strength within us, that empowers us to withstand and navigate through the most intense impacts of trauma without completely breaking down. It is this intrinsic ability to consistently realign our spirit's vibrations into fresh states of stability as we adapt to the ongoing seismic shocks and internal disruptions caused by life's unpredictable events. This unwavering resilience is truly what enables us to not just survive but thrive in the face of adversity.

Post-traumatic growth represents the deeply profound and transformative outcome that emerges when our resilient core actively incorporates every challenge into a continuously expanding, enlightened self-architecture. It is the ecstatic quantum essence of our existence, sprouting from the ashes of resilience to unfurl an entirely new narrative of brilliance crafted specifically for this current hero's journey.

This profound journey of holistic embodied reclamation is the sacred path we have fearlessly illuminated together - courageously choosing to no longer suppress or evade the profound impacts of trauma on every facet of our being. Through this transformative process, we embrace the art of compassionately rewriting and acknowledging all physical, mental, energetic, and behavioral manifestations that surface in the wake of upheaval.

By fully allowing ourselves to experience and make sense of the impacts on our mind and body, we start to see the deeper underlying patterns and roots of our trauma responses. What once felt like disconnected reactions start fitting together in an understandable way. As we stay present with the disturbances happening within us, however uncomfortable, we gain a clearer sense of our core selves and what we need to reorient in a healthier direction.

This profound and transformative journey that we have embarked on together has been nothing short of a sacred exploration into the depths of our beings. We have learned to decipher the intricate imprints of trauma that have left their mark on us, recognizing them not as scars but as divine messages calling us to embark on a journey of self-realization. These encrypted invitations beckon us to navigate through uncharted territories of our own existence, urging us to focus on our inner myths and poetic truths with unwavering dedication. As we embrace this cosmic call to rediscover ourselves as mystic phoenixes rising from the ashes, we are reminded of the inherent glory and boundless potential that lies within each of us.

Those initial phases of fallout can feel like being violently thrust into a cyclone of bewilderment, fear, and soul-shuddering grief. For some, this sense of living in trauma's eclipsed shadow may mercifully pass in a relatively brief span. While for others, the disorientation of having our previously sun-soaked existence suddenly extinguished can stretch into what feels like an endless void without escape.

No matter how long or brief these periods of darkness and struggle feel, they are not a permanent condition or a punishment. They are temporary transitional phases we have to move through. As painful as it is in those moments, these are transformative experiences that break down the unhealthy coping mechanisms and self-limiting beliefs that previously defined us. Going through this is what allows our truest, most liberated selves to finally emerge.

So, when you feel consumed by sorrow's haunting echoes or caught in cycles of inner chaos, return to this grounded breath. The skills and practices planted are not just markers for wading through darkness, but jewels activating the courage and vision required for your soul's healing and transformation.

Those mindfulness meditations, self-compassion rituals, and other modalities are now interwoven into your very being—map codes steadily remembering your essence's infinite energy and radiance. They are the lucid voices prompting you to keep forging ahead with fierce grace when obstacles or setbacks cloud the way forward.

You have already ignited the flame of heroic perseverance within you, empowering yourself to stride confidently along the path of eternal rebirth and continuous self-discovery. Now, embrace and respect this enchanting process of manifesting your dreams with steadfast patience. Record each moment of resurgence with meticulous care as you demonstrate your unwavering dedication to healing and growth.

Faith has been another game-changer on this journey, though we all have to find that soul-nourishing source in our own way. I'm talking about mustering that deep-down trust that things will ultimately realign, even when our minds can't rationally map out the how's and whys. Faith gifts us the grit to keep showing up through the chaos until those sacred reshufflings our spirits have conspired to bring about finally click into a clear place.

Maybe for you, that unwavering belief system stems from religious or spiritual traditions that remind you of the benevolent orders underlying presence. Or perhaps it's more an unshakable faith in your own heroic development - that no matter how hot the metamorphic fires get, you'll keep emerging as the radiant truth you've been coded for since birth. Either way, find what replenishes your childlike awe at the wildly exciting unknown. Let that wonderment be your lifeline through any lingering doubt.

I can't stress enough how vital that outer circle of relationships also is for sustaining you. Whether that's the unconditional acceptance of family who'll bear witness to your every unedited truth without flinching. The kindred spirits who'll counsel you from their experience unwinding similar inner knots. Or sage therapeutic allies skilled at tending to the most volcanic explosions as you rebirth the multi-dimensional aspects of your most self.

You require individuals who will unwaveringly stand by your side during even the most challenging and tumultuous moments when you feel like you are losing touch with your true self. These souls possess unwavering compassion, creating a safe haven for you to navigate through the chaos of self-discovery and transformation. They patiently hold space for your personal growth until you emerge like the magnificent phoenix we keep talking about, shedding old layers and revealing a glorious new version of yourself. It is paramount that you surround yourself with these essential kaleidoscopic mirrors, reflecting back the beauty and strength that lies within you.

The honest truth is, you are destined for profound personal transformation. Not just someday in the distant future, but starting right now, in this present moment. Your most authentic, unleashed self is striving to fully emerge. This process requires you to go through many difficult transitions and upheavals, but that is part of arriving at your most genuine expression of who you are in an intimate and powerful way.

Stay confidently rooted in awe as you navigate through the storms of life, always moving towards a harmonious reunion with your true self. Embrace the transformative process even when your familiar self-concepts crumble and you find yourself in a state of uncertainty. Trust this journey as a testament to your inner strength and resilience. It signifies the dissolution of old patterns that no longer serve you, paving the way for new cosmic revelations to manifest within you with unparalleled grace and wisdom.

Stay committed to unconditionally loving yourself in every transformative moment - and the undeniable power that you have always sensed simmering just beneath the surface will undoubtedly manifest its most glorious visions and profound expressions of a deeply fulfilling return to your authentic self. Embrace this truth with every fiber of your being, as each radiant spark of universal energy has been intricately woven into the tapestry of your continuous journey towards rediscovering your divine spirit and self-realization. Trust in this process with unwavering faith, for it is a sacred reunion with the infinite source of love and joy that resides within you.

Encouraging Ongoing Growth: Staying Committed to Personal Development

You know, just when we think we've finally cracked the code on integrating all these hard-won wisdom tools and we start relaxing in our fresh resurgence, life's got a funny way of throwing new chaotic twisters our way to keep leveling us up.

Those once rock-solid coping strategies that felt like such soul-anchors during the last tsunami? They'll absolutely still be vital vibrational medicine for years to come. But the real test lies in whether we stay devoted to actively evolving our personal growth practices as we continually rebirth into unexpected versions of ourselves.

Because mark my words - just when you think you've finally wrestled your most harrowing demons into submission, a fresh hell will rear its metaphorical head. Could be an unexpected health crisis, the molting of a pivotal relationship, or simply getting walloped by an intense resurgence of old trauma triggers we thought were laid to rest.

The point is that this whole human development experience is one infinitely evolving improvisation after another. We never truly "arrive" at some final decoded self that gets to plant roots forever. Treacherous plot twist whirlwinds continuously plot to uproot us from our comfort zones and thrust us into fertile new frontiers of growth, ready or not.

So, while staunchly clinging to what has worked thus far isn't just permissible, it's absolutely vital for anchoring our spirits throughout such disruptions. We've also had to commit to staying endlessly curious, adaptive, and devoted to refining the most alchemic rituals and soul-fortifying practices for orienting ourselves amidst each recalibration.

One of the most pragmatic yet potent ways to ritualize this lifelong journey of metamorphosis? Keep refining your inspired-to-the-soul goal setting and achievement processes based on what most enthusiastically lights you up here and now.

I'm talking about continually checking in with your heart's deepest callings, then reverse-engineering those big picture vision quests into bite-sized cementing rituals to integrate one steady step at a time. Not just allowing priorities to inadvertently drift based on circumstances, but powerfully re-authoring the gateways your growth truly craves.

This could mean regularly re-evaluating your career goals as new interests emerge, finding new ways to strengthen your relationships and feel more fulfilled, or envisioning an entirely new path for expressing your talents and passions. Whatever your evolving desires are, get clear on exactly what you want by vividly picturing it in detail. Then start breaking it down into concrete, manageable steps that will help you progressively work toward fully embodying that vision.

The key lies in treating this goal-crafting process not as some perfunctory productivity hustle but as an intimate self-attunement ritual in itself. It is a ceremonial getting naked with your evolving essence and negotiating the most mutually orgasmic pathways forward for you to thrive. Then, stick to those realignments with unwavering yet playful devotion, allowing each incremental "win" to illuminate the next inspired unveiling.

In the grand tapestry of life, each one of us is a divine being on an eternal journey of self-discovery and self-realization. We are like demigods, gradually awakening to the profound essence of our existence and learning how to luxuriously savor the experience of being our true selves. So, why not embrace the joycus task of documenting and manifesting our most glorious transformation into an ecstatic lifelong adventure? It is an opportunity to revel in the splendor of our rebirth and celebrate the magical unfolding of our highest potential.

Okay, so we've gotten radically honest about those catalytic areas ripe for your next level-ups, whether fortifying emotional resilience, upgrading core self-worth codes, or beta-testing fresh coping flows. Now it's time to start mapping these inspirations from their etheric blueprints into tangible, bite-sized quests of desire actualization.

We're talking about putting that goal-crafting process through its metaphysical power-up by enmeshing it with the whole SMART goals cocktail - Specificity, Measurable, Achievable, Relevant, and Time-Bound goals. Your personal growth should go beyond just wishful thinking or vague ideas. It needs to take shape as a concrete, structured process of real, tangible progress towards an elevated state of being. This involves making substantive shifts, not just in your outer circumstances and actions, but in your inner mindset, energy, and sense of self.

For example, instead of simply setting a vague goal of "improving self-worth," you could strategically deconstruct this ambitious mission into manageable, time-blocked projects. Embrace the role of a master illusionist's apprentice, committing to a dedicated practice for the next 28 days. Envision yourself dedicating x minutes each day to deeply instilling new self-appreciation mantras and empowering rituals upon waking and before drifting off at night. Elevate your psychospiritual arsenal, ensuring that each milestone is satisfactorily anchored before progressing to the next level of skills acquisition. Monitor these enhancements closely, fine-tuning them as needed to experience a tangible sense of progress and personal growth within yourself.

From this starting point, you could envision and design your very own innovative twist on the timeless methodology - perhaps by integrating enriching rewards that align with specific achievement milestones. Picture indulging your inner authority with regular, indulgent magnificently curated experiences each time you achieve a set number of consecutive days practicing self-care rituals. Alternatively, treat yourself to a day of spontaneous creative exploration whenever you surpass a particular productivity goal or aspiration.

The essence of personal growth lies in tailoring strategies and methods that deeply resonate with you. It involves integrating these approaches with your unique psychological and spiritual creativity, crafting paths that align with your personal journey and the specific challenges you're destined to navigate. Embrace unconventional thinking in your developmental process, ensuring each step is a triumphant evolution towards becoming a more vibrant and victorious version of yourself.

Growth is always guiding you toward expressing your true, uninhibited essence. As you develop new skills, expand your awareness, and integrate powerful insights, you are fulfilling the original promise of your cosmic birth, emerging transformed from the chrysalis of your own evolution.

Fully dedicate yourself to refining your personal growth practices until they feel just right for you. Approach life as the epic, wildly extraordinary journey of transformation that it is meant to be. Begin wherever and whenever feels most exciting and celebrate each milestone along the way as a momentous achievement in its own right.

Immersing yourself in materials focused on post-traumatic growth can also be a game changer. I'm talking about diving into those books, articles, videos— anything that can shed more light on the real-life journeys of people who've walked this path before you. Hearing their tales of triumphing over the darkest chapters and growing in unexpected ways? That's fuel for realizing you've got an entire audience cheering you on from the other side of these trials.

Because here's the thing - trauma tries really hard to convince us that we're alone, terminally stuck in our personal apocalypse with no way out. But surrounding yourself with the empowering narratives and wisdom from these post-traumatic trailblazers is a constant reminder that your healing and growth is not just possible but hardwired into your DNA as a ridiculously resilient human being.

You'll gain insights into navigating the messiness from new angles, hopeful perspectives on maintaining progress over the long term, and inspiration for finding those silver linings we often can't see in the heart of the storm itself. Reading these lived testimonies is like gifting yourself a supportive crew whispering, "You've so got this". Look how many others found their healed selves after journeying through their own fresh hells."

And can we get real about the sheer cathartic medicine that comes from you sharing your own hardscrabble adventures out there too? The simple act of openly storytelling your saga to those who need to hear it somehow makes the wounds feel lighter to carry, you know? Like exhaling a long-held breath and realizing the next inhalation gets to be that much sweeter and truer to your post-traumatic rebirth.

Because you're doing so much more than providing comfort to others still wading through their own shadow-beginnings when you let those words pour out unedited. You're honoring your ability to reframe each trauma storyline from its original vantage of disempowered victimhood into a hero's journey it's always been coded to serve from the start.

Each recounting births more breaths into the empowered change you're feverishly summoning into manifestation through this whole weird, messy, sacred process. And as the narrative transforms under your autonomous re-storying abilities, you inevitably rewrite the very personal identities and self-beliefs those old winding tales once kept bounded within their limiting grips.

Final Words of Inspiration: Motivational Guidance for the Road Ahead

As I sit here putting the final touches on this journey, waves of emotion are washing over me. For years, the dream of taking my experiences and transforming them into something that could help guide others felt both vitally important yet totally out of reach. A part of me worried that the shattered fragments of who I used to be were too broken, too incoherent, to ever be woven into something of real value.

But here we are - a truth made manifest that I've not only survived the un-survivable, but now get to redefine the entire trajectory of who I become from those sacred ashes. Getting these words out of my heart's tangled depths and onto these pages has sparked a profound clarity for my soul, an unfurling release of pent-up wisdom longing to finally be exhaled into form.

And in rising to meet this creative challenge, I've realized an unshakable knowing: that the supposed "life sentence" of trauma I once felt condemned to was actually serving a far more healing purpose. By courageously refusing to accept those limiting storylines thrust upon my innocence, I opened a portal into learning how to truly love and realize my intrinsic enoughness.

Yes, clawing back that retrieval of self-worth has involved treading through my fair share of shattered dreams and bone-deep inner bruising. Make no mistake, there have been plenty of seemingly endless voids where despair had me in a vice grip and I genuinely couldn't see a way to keep going.

But something primal within refused to surrender. Call it resilience, divinely coded perseverance, my soul's ferocious commitment to unleashing itself into full bloom - whatever you want to name that animating lifeforce, I chose to dig in and consciously nurture its growth over my momentarily extinguished spirits.

And that's the elemental ceremony I'm extending to you now, with every hard-won revelation contained in these pages: an invitation to go inward and excavate your own heart's underground streams of unbreakable courage. To honor the inevitability of overwhelming segments by staking your worth not on sprinting through them, but on making the choice to keep leaning into your becoming no matter how arduous the labor.

Because listen - I don't just believe in your capacity to rise from trauma's ashes into the most awesome revelations of your highest self...I'm certain of it. You've been encoded with profound gifts akin to wildflowers reseeding after every forest fire, equipped with the instinctual wisdom to perpetually rebirth into more fundamental truth telling of your soul.

Keep reorienting yourself towards that timeless resilience, taking each step with a fierceness that can only be forged by those who've walked through the hottest fires. You have everything required to reclaim your heroic narrative of healing, growth and unwavering self-realization. All that's needed now is to keep moving steadfastly into fuller embodiment of that truth.

But remember, you don't have to walk this path alone. Lean into those supportive circles, whether that's beloved friends and relatives who've earned the right to bear witness or professionals specially trained to nurture you through the heavy energies. Have no shame in reaching out for their caring anchors when the way forward feels obscured. With patience, compassion for your process, and a collection of echoing presences cheering you onward, you will absolutely emerge from this transformative fire into the most transcendent versions of your truth yet to bloom.

Because the reality is, even your most glowing selfhoods awaiting manifestation are far more capable and resilient than you likely allow yourself to feel in your rawer human space. You've been coded with mythic insights, phoenix DNA if you will, and a primal instinct to perpetually rebirth yourself into wider fields of light no matter how intense the fires get. That heroic fortitude is literally written into every subatomic fiber of your being.

Have unwavering trust in the unchangeable frequencies that are intricately woven into the fabric of the universe, all working harmoniously towards manifesting your highest potential. Maintain a relentless sense of optimism by grounding yourself in the profound wisdom that lies deep within your soul, affirming that your future brilliance is not merely a possibility but a destined certainty eagerly anticipating its cosmic alignment with your authentic self in all its magnificent and unrestrained forms.

This whole experience has simply been a ceremonial unfolding to purify the most obstructed beliefs and ancestral scarring, aligning you into successively clarified courses of your sovereignty's unstoppable contentment—endlessly refining your selfhood into an unflinchingly electric authenticity.

Thus, the road from here can absolutely feel daunting because of our limited human predictions. Rocky, seemingly endless seasons of developing into the tender vulnerabilities you've been conditioned to guard so fiercely for so long. But mark these words - every single seeming dead-end is merely the infinite hallway bending you back into the core truth of your spirit's most legendary reveling yet. Each brutally honest unfurlment a victorious unlocking into exponentially more liberated, self-celebratory rebirth.

Summon that raw, persistent heroic soul within you, brave one, as you embark on the exhilarating journey ahead. Embrace the unwavering certainty that you are continuously evolving towards profound revelations of wholeness, even amidst the tumultuous and disorienting twists and turns of life's challenges. Each tender yet brutal excavation serves to dismantle barriers and filters, paving the way for your most boldly empowered experiences to shine through with magnificent clarity.

Within the confines of these pages lie profound love-maps designed to guide you through the turbulent journey of self-discovery. Yet, beyond these words, in the untamed areas of uncharted territories waiting to be discovered, your soul's most awe-inspiring revelations eagerly await being unlocked and unleashed. This is where a boundless multiverse of your eternal transformation begins - right here, right now - with each cautious stride leading you towards embracing the majestic, unyielding magnificence that has always been destined for you to enthusiastically embody and ultimately transform into reality.

Believe in yourself wholeheartedly because I believe in you. Take back your power and create the life you so deserve because a magnificent life awaits you beyond the scars.

Heal, so you don't have to give a sarcastic tone to uplifting messages. Heal, so you never have to make anyone else the object of your own frustration. Heal, so when someone tells you they love you, you may allow yourself to believe them.

~ Banff Wellness Retreat

www.ingramcontent.com/pod-product-compliance
Lightning Source LLC
Chambersburg PA
CBHW031415120626
46545CB00006B/2142